DENVER
HIKING GUIDE
45 TRAILS WITHIN 45 MINUTES OF DENVER

3D PRESS, INC.

3D PRESS, INC.
4340 E. KENTUCKY AVE., SUITE 446
DENVER, CO 80246
888-456-3607
info@3dpress.net / www.3dpress.net

ISBN 1-889593-58-3

PRINTED IN THE U.S.A.

Forward

Hiking is a wonderful sport for everyone, from young children to their greatgrandparents, and generations can enjoy it together for years. Hiking offers an excellent aerobic workout, and the opportunity to breathe pure mountain air, listen to birds sing, watch hawks soar and perhaps even catching a glimpse of a deer or a Rocky Mountain Big Horn Sheep. Hiking can also serve to introduce children to the pleasures of Colorado's outdoors, instilling a lifelong interest in and respect for nature and physical fitness.

The *Denver Hiking Guide* has trails for all abilities, 45 in all, from short, flat dirt paths you can cover in an hour or less, to day-long tromps through the foothills or to the summit of a 12,000 foot peak. Best of all, most of these hikes can all be found within a 45 minute drive of many points in the city.

Each trail in this guide includes driving directions and drive time to the trailhead, a detailed route description and map, many optional routes enabling you to tailor the hike to the length and difficulty desired, elevation gain graph, a difficulty rating and, unique to this guide, recommendations, options and descriptions of each route for trail runners and families with young children.

Acknowledgements

Thanks go to the following people whose help made this book possible: My parents, Robert and Myra Rich for their encouragement, advice and editing, and for the descriptions of the Chief Mountain and Beaver Trails; Jocelyn Cree for cover design; Erica Schaumberg for the area map on pages 6-7; Trails Illustrated, the U.S. Forest Service, Jefferson County Open Space, the South Suburban Recreation District, the Lakewood Parks Department and the Colorado State Parks for the use of their maps; and the Denver Public Library's History Archive for the black and white photos that adorn the interior of the book.

Introduction

The ski area rating system is used to symbolize the difficulty of each trail.

● An easier trail – most anyone can do it. Appropriate for families. Generally smooth with little elevation change.

■ For people in relatively good shape with some hiking experience. Some rocky or steep sections.

◆ For experienced hikers in very good to excellent shape. With steep or technically difficult sections.

Because hiking is an aerobic activity, start with a hike at or below what you consider to be your level and progress from there.

Trail Rules

1 **Stay on the Trail** At high altitude, the ecosystem is fragile, easily damaged and takes years to heal.

2 **Pack Out At Least As Much As You Pack In.**

3 **Never Startle Animals** Stop and let animals move away from the trail, then pass slowly.

4 **Yield The Trail** Horses are easily scared. Always stop, move off the trail and let them pass.

5 **Respect Closed Areas** Do not trespass on private lands or hike on closed trails. If you are not sure if a trail is open, ask first!

Essentials

1 **Altitude Sickness** This can be a serious problem. If you are coming from low altitude, give yourself a chance to acclimate and do not over-exert during your first few days at high altitude. Drink plenty of water; this will help a lot! Symptoms of altitude sickness include nausea, dizziness and headaches. The best remedy, if possible, is to return to a lower elevation as quickly as possible.

2 **Do Not Drink Untreated Water Out Of Any Stream or Lake! Giardia is Common in Untreated Water.**

3 **Food and Drink** Bring at least one quart of water per person. Food isn't a necessity but you'll be glad to have some. Good hiking snacks include energy bars, trail mix, apples and anything else that travels well, is easily digested and is high in carbohydrates. With kids, food and drink is a must (for their happines and yours!).

4 **Clothing** The main idea is *be prepared*! Weather changes rapidly in the mountains. Getting caught in a storm at 10,000 feet is not only unpleasant, but can be dangerous as well. Hypothermia is a threat, even in summer, and it can snow during any month of the year at higher altitudes. Always bring a good raincoat and an extra shirt. Other musts at altitude are sunscreen and sunglasses; the sun is much more intense at high altitude (Every 1,000 feet gained in elevation increases the exposure to harmful rays by 4%).

Trail Directory

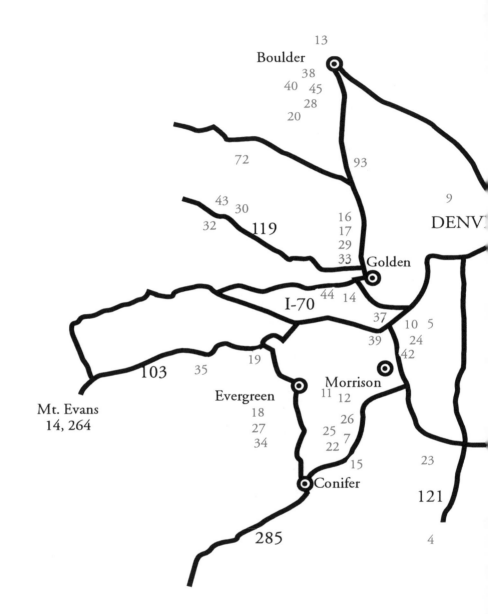

Boulder   13

38

40   45

28

20

72   93

9

DENV

43   30

32   119

16
17
29
33   Golden

I-70   44   14

37

10   5

39   24

42

103   35   19   Morrison

Evergreen   11   12

Mt. Evans
14, 264

18

27

34

26

25   7

22

15

23

Conifer

121

285   4

6

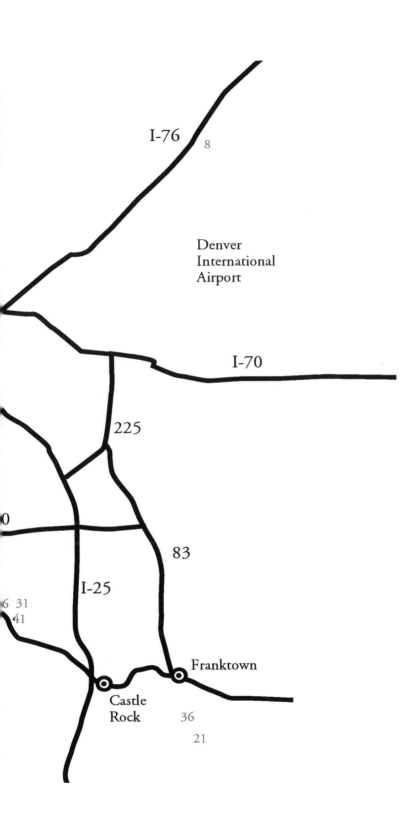

I-76   8

Denver
International
Airport

I-70

225

0

83

I-25

6 31
41

Franktown

Castle
Rock   36

21

Highline Canal
North End

Distance	2.4-4 miles
Elevation Gain	0-50 ft
High Point	5465 ft
Difficulty	●
Terrain	Wide Trail
Bikes	Moderate
Dogs	Leashed

ELEVATION

No Significant Elevation Change

MILES

Trail Intro The Highline Canal is a flat dirt path the width of a single lane road. Open to hikers, horses and bikes, it's a quiet riparian retreat from the suburban sprawl of the southern metroplex.

Part 1: Colorado to Dahlia (2.4 miles)
Trail Intro This section heads southeast behind Cherry Hills mansions and is a quick getaway from the city. For a longer hike, you can continue across Quincy for as long as you want (Bellview is another 1.5 miles past Dahlia).
Access Drive south on I-25 to Colorado Blvd. Turn south on Colorado Blvd. Past Hampden, Colorado Blvd. becomes a quiet two-lane street. .7 miles past Hampden look for trail parking on your left.

Part 2: Dahlia to Bellview (3.0 miles)
Trail Intro The stretch is particularly nice, heading south past the wildlife refuge behind my alma mater, Kent Denver School, and into more country-like areas of horses, grass-lands and panoramic views of the Front Range.
Access Drive south on I-25 to Colorado Blvd. Turn south (right) on Colorado and drive past Hampden to its end at Quincy. Turn left and continue to Dahlia (the next stop sign). Turn right and drive to Dahlia's end where it intersects the Highline Canal.

Part 3: Orchard Road to University Blvd. (3.7 miles)
Trail Intro A shady section with horse farms and little traffic.
Access Drive south on I-25 and turn south on University. At Orchard Road, turn left (east) and then take your first left (on the street opposite the shopping center). Then take your first right onto Long Road. Follow Long Road around, it turns back into Orchard Road. Orchard Road crosses over the Highline Canal and there is a parking lot on your left.

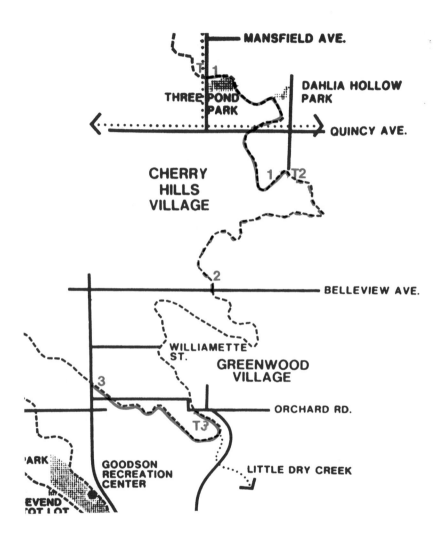

MANSFIELD AVE.

T1

DAHLIA HOLLOW PARK

THREE POND PARK

QUINCY AVE.

CHERRY HILLS VILLAGE

1 T2

2

BELLEVIEW AVE.

WILLIAMETTE ST.

GREENWOOD VILLAGE

3

ORCHARD RD.

T3

PARK

GOODSON RECREATION CENTER

LITTLE DRY CREEK

EVEND OT LOT

Distance	3-5.4 miles
Elevation Gain	0 ft
High Point	5450 ft
Difficulty	●
Terrain	Wide Trail
Bikes	Moderate
Dogs	Leashed

2 / Highline Canal South End

E
L
E
V
A
T
I
O
N

No Significant Elevation Change

M I L E S

Trail Intro The Highline Canal is a flat, dirt path the width of a narrow road, open to hikers, horses and bikes. It is a quiet riparian retreat from the suburban sprawl of the southern metroplex.

Part 4: Goodson Rec. Center to Franklin (4.0 miles)
Trail Intro A nice stroll that wanders southwest past horse farms and mountain vistas, and into dense, green river habitat.
Access Drive south on I-25 to University. Turn south (right) and drive to the South Suburban/Goodson Rec. Center (.5 miles south of Orchard Road) and park there.

Part 5: Windermere to Freemont (2.8-3.8 miles)
Part 6: Windermere to Mineral (2.0 miles)
Trail Intro Two short walks that cross no major streets and are thus ideal for families. (Freemont is not shown on the map, but is between Broadway and Lee Gulch Trail. You can add an extra mile by continuing to Ridge Road (within sight of Broadway and a strip mall) and then returning.)
Access Drive south on I-25 to Sante Fe. Turn south (right) on Sante Fe. Turn left on Prince (the first light after Bellview) and follow it for 1.4 miles to Ridge Road. Turn left, continue 1.9 miles and turn right on Windermere (at a 4-way stop). Drive .9 miles and park at the trail, just after a "Narrow Bridge" sign.

Part 7: County Line Road to Mineral (2.0 miles)
Trail Intro A great family walk with excellent mountain views. The trail goes north from County Line Road to Mineral. The only street crossing is the initial dash across County Line Road.
Access Drive south on I-25. Exit at Sante Fe Drive south. Drive south to County Line Road (the last street before C-470), turn left and continue 1.8 miles to the trail parking, which is on your right.

For more information call South Suburban Park and Recreation District at 798-2493.

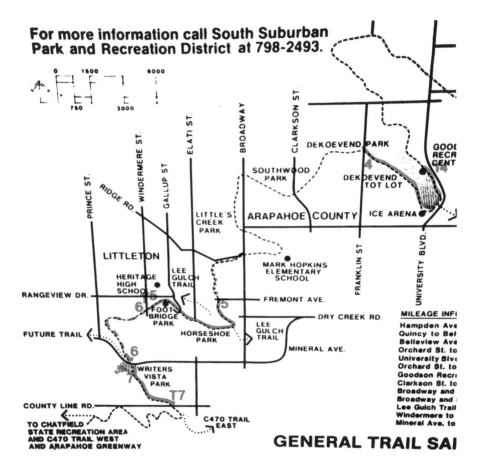

GENERAL TRAIL SAI

MILEAGE INFO
Hampden Ave
Quincy to Bel
Belleview Ave
Orchard St. to
University Blvo
Orchard St. to
Goodson Recr
Clarkson St. to
Broadway and
Broadway and
Lee Gulch Trail
Windermere to
Mineral Ave. to

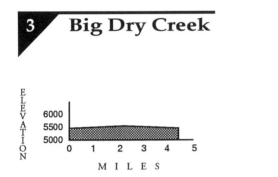

Distance	4.4 miles
Elevation Gain	85 ft
High Point	5,525 ft
Difficulty	●
Terrain	Trail
Bikes	Light
Dogs	Leashed

Trail Intro One of the least 'urban' feeling of the inner-city trails, it crosses a park, then follows Big Dry Creek to its end. The trail is sheltered from the houses along the route by tall cottonwoods, making it not only more pleasant but keeping it cool on hot summer days.

Access Drive south on I-25 and exit on University Blvd south. Drive south on University to the South Suburban/Goodson Rec. Center (.5 miles south of Orchard Road) and park there.
Drive Time 30 minutes

The Hike Join the Highline Canal Trail and walk a couple hundred yards south (toward Franklin St.). Turn left onto the Big Dry Creek Trail, which starts with a bridge crossing. Walk through Cherry Knolls Park and continue along this winding trail as it parallels Big Dry Creek to its end at Colorado Blvd. and South Suburban Golf Course. Return as you came.

Trail Running A nice run for beginning trail runners with little elevation change, nice scenery and lots of shady cottonwoods.

With the Kids Perfect for the family. Wide, smooth trails and you can turn around at any point. Cherry Knolls Park is about .5 miles from the trailhead and has water and a playground.

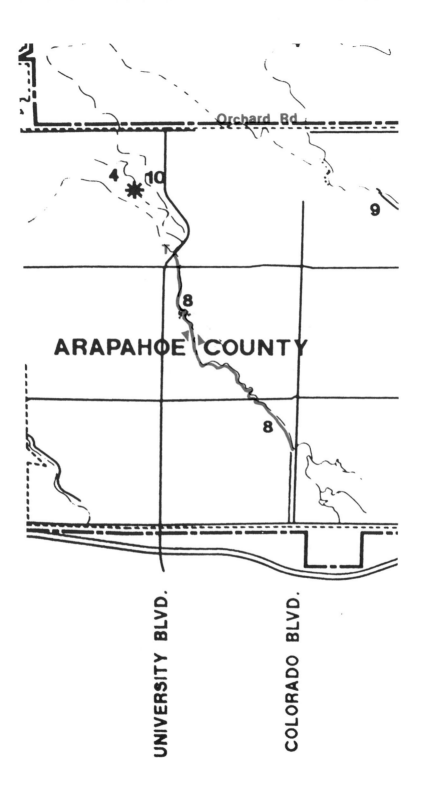

Orchard Rd

4 10

9

8

ARAPAHOE COUNTY

8

UNIVERSITY BLVD.

COLORADO BLVD.

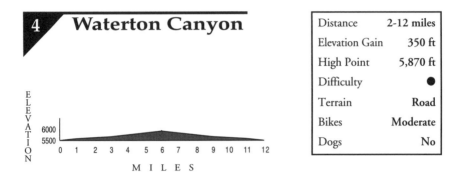

4 Waterton Canyon		
Distance	2-12 miles
Elevation Gain	350 ft
High Point	5,870 ft
Difficulty	●
Terrain	Road
Bikes	Moderate
Dogs	No

Trail Intro A beautiful canyon with many species of wildlife, including an occasionally seen herd of big horn sheep near the trailhead. Many people bring a fishing rod and cast their way up and back along this stretch of the South Platte.

Access from I-25 and 6th Ave. Drive west on 6th Ave., turn south on Wadsworth and drive to its intersection with C-470. Staying on Wadsworth, go under C-470, drive 5 miles and turn left on the Waterton Canyon/Roxborough State Park road, just before Martin Marietta. Take your second left into the big parking lot.
Drive Time 35 minutes

The Hike Carefully cross the road and begin following the dirt, road-width trail. Go through a gate, next to an outhouse, and enter the canyon. The trail parallels the river for 6 miles up to the Waterton Canyon dam, but you can turn around at any point. There are picnic tables and rest rooms at the trailhead and at the dam.

Trail Running A potentially long (half-marathon length, if you run to the Colorado Trail trailhead), though relatively flat run up a pretty canyon on a wide dirt road. The canyon can be searing at mid-day in summer, but cools down quickly when the sun dips behind the canyon walls.

With the Kids With the road being closed to motor vehicles and wide enough to easily accommodate all trail-users, Waterton Canyon is a good family hike. There is a picnic area just past the trailhead among shady cottonwood trees.

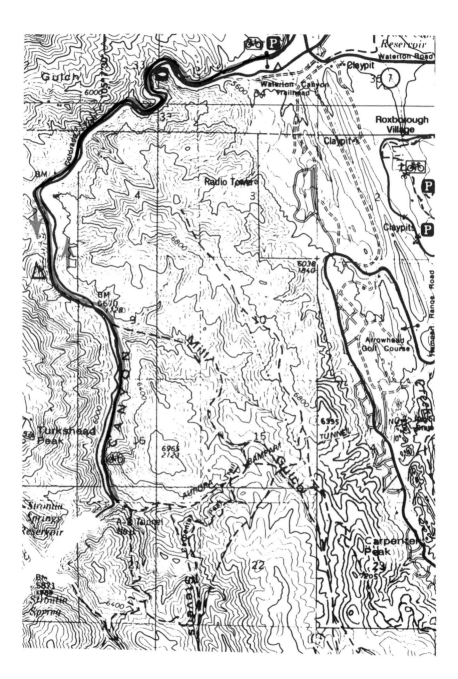

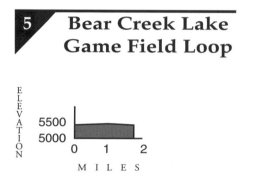

5 Bear Creek Lake Game Field Loop

Distance	1.7-3 miles
Elevation Gain	50 ft
High Point	5,465 ft
Difficulty	●
Terrain	Trail
Bikes	Light
Dogs	Leashed

Trail Intro A well marked loop along Bear Creek with 20 different fitness stations.

Access from I-25 and 6th Ave. Drive west on 6th to Kipling. Turn south, travel 4.4 miles to Morrison Road/Hwy. 8 and turn right (west). In 3.7 miles, turn left into Bear Creek Lake Park. Immediately turn left again, drive past the entrance gate and turn right at the stop sign, following the sign for the Park Office. In .6 miles, turn left, again toward the Park Office. In .8 miles, turn left, away from the Park Office, and continue to the end of the road and the start of the fitness trail, which is on the left side of the lot. **Drive Time** 25 minutes

The Hike Follow the fitness trail in a counterclockwise loop. You can tack on an additional 1.3 miles by adding the Bear Creek Lake Trail (#10) to the loop. Join the trail that takes off from the midpoint between fitness stations 9 and 10. Walk .1 miles and you will see the bridge described in the Bear Creek Lake Trail. Continue past the bridge and follow the directions for the Bear Creek Lake Trail (#10) to the point where it crosses the bridge. Here, turn left and rejoin the Game Field Loop.

Trail Running A flat run with 20 fitness stations. You can make the run up to 3 miles by tacking on the Bear Creek Lake Trail (#10), as described above in The Hike.

For Families An easy, lightly traveled trail, though I prefer the Bear Creek Lake Trail (#10) for a family walk.

Trail Notes It costs $3 to enter Bear Creek Lake Park.

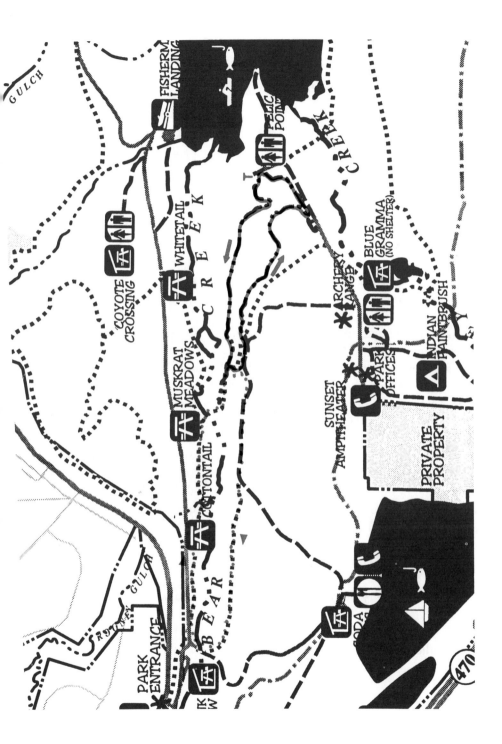

Map by Lakewood Parks

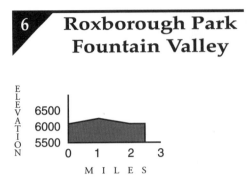

Distance	2.5 miles
Elevation Gain	210 ft
High Point	6,415 ft
Difficulty	●
Terrain	Wide Trail
Bikes	No
Dogs	No

Trail Intro An easy, self-guided nature walk with 20 signed interpretive stops on a wide trail. The loop travels the north end of Roxborough Park, among the spectacular "flatiron" red rock formations for which the park is so well known.

Access from I-25 and 6th Ave. Drive west on 6th Ave. to Wadsworth, turn south and follow it past C-470. 5 miles past C-470, turn left following the signs for Roxborough Park. Immediately bear left again, continuing to the road's end at Rampart Range Road. Turn right and follow the signs for another 4.4 miles to the Roxborough Park visitor's center parking lot.
Drive Time 45 minutes

The Hike Turn right out of the visitor's center and join the Fountain Valley Trail. Pass the Fountain Valley Overlook and stay right at a junction, following a counterclockwise loop of the nature trail. Be sure to include a side hike to the Lyons Overlook with its views of the amazing, jutting red sandstone Lyons and Fountain formations that are the park's hallmark. The backside of the loop passes between these formations affording a close-up view of this unique Front Range feature.

Trail Running Pretty short. Try Roxborough Park – South Rim Trail (#31) instead.

For Families An educational stroll among the beautiful red rocks. To be avoided on hot days

Trail Notes It costs $5 to enter Roxborough State Park. Guide books for the interpretive trail are available for sale at the visitor's center for $1.

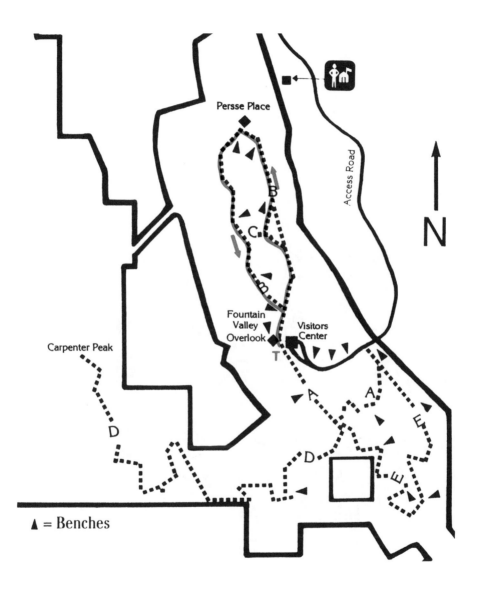

Persse Place

Access Road

B

C

D

N

Carpenter Peak

Fountain
Valley
Overlook

Visitors
Center

T

A

A

E

D

D

E

A

▲ = Benches

Fountain Valley, Roxborough State Park

Photo © Denver Public Library - Western History Department

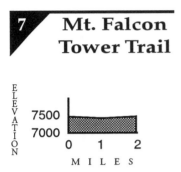

Distance	2.0 miles
Elevation Gain	100 ft
High Point	7,535 ft
Difficulty	●
Terrain	Trail
Bikes	Heavy
Dogs	Leashed

Trail Intro An easy hike good for children and those of us not in as good of shape as we'd like to be; it's short, doesn't gain much elevation and is on wide dirt paths. The Eagle's Eye Shelter has a roof, benches and tables for picnicking, and great views to the west and south. In summer, the backside of the loop, along the Meadow View Trail, is ablaze with sunflowers, Indian Paintbrush, Butter and Eggs, and myriad other wildflowers.

Access from 6th Ave. and I-70 Drive west on 6th Ave. to I-70. Drive .5 miles west on I-70 and turn south on C-470. Turn south again onto Hwy. 285. Drive 4.2 miles up Turkey Creek Canyon and turn right on Parmalee Road, marked with a brown sign for Mt. Falcon. Drive up Parmalee Road, following the signs to the park.
Drive Time 40 minutes

The Hike Begin on the road-width Castle Trail. Pass the Parmalee Trail and turn right on the Meadow Trail. At the next junction, continue straight up the Tower Trail. The Eagle's Eye Shelter is on your right about 100 yards up. After stopping at this great view point, continue up to the fire lookout tower. From there, it's a gentle descent on a wide trail. At the Meadow View Trail, turn left, walk to the Castle Trail, turn left and return to the start.

Trail Running Pretty short. Try the Ft. Falcon – Devil's Elbow Trail (#22) instead; it covers the same terrain and totals nearly 4 miles.

For Families A nice walk with a rest area at the Eagle's Eye Shelter where you could have a picnic, and wildflower covered meadows.

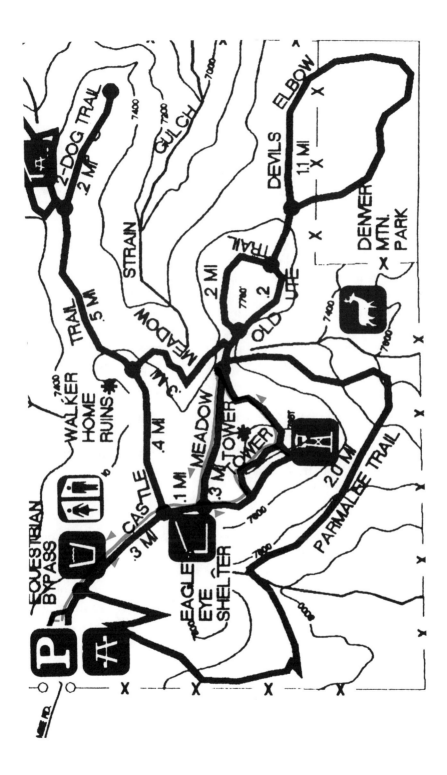

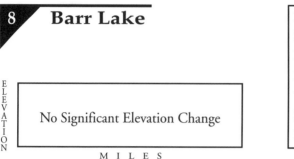

Distance	3.0 miles
Elevation Gain	0 ft
High Point	5,280 ft
Difficulty	●
Terrain	Road/Trail
Bikes	No
Dogs	No

Trail Intro This easy hike follows an unused road and a boardwalk, which travels out over the lake, leading to the wildlife refuge established on one end of the 1,600 acre Barr Lake. This is a great hike for families and anyone else interested in seeing the largest variety of wildlife along the Front Range, and visiting a wonderful nature center. Viewing "blinds" have been erected for spying on the many species of birds and mammals living along the shore. The hike ends at a gazebo built perched above the water, 200 feet from the shore.

Access from I-25 and 6th Ave. Drive north on I-25 and then turn east on I-76, toward Ft. Morgan. Follow I-76 for 16.7 miles to exit 216 (Bromley Lane). Turn right, drive 1.2 miles to Picadilly Road, marked by a sign for Barr Lake State Park, and turn right. In 1.9 miles, enter the park and follow the road to the Nature Center.
Drive Time 35 minutes

The Hike From the nature center, turn left on the Nature Trail and follow it around the lake. There are two viewing blinds along the way, before the walk ends in 1.5 miles at the gazebo. Spend some time here looking west using the viewing telescope provided by the park as you get a great look at Long's Peak, the Front Range and numerous nesting sites, including an eagle's, in the cottonwood trees on the western shore of the lake.

Trail Running A flat 9 mile dirt road loop of the lake is your only option; not bad for a distance run and very tranquil.

With Kids A superb outdoor educational experience.

Trail Notes It costs $5 to enter Barr Lake State Park.

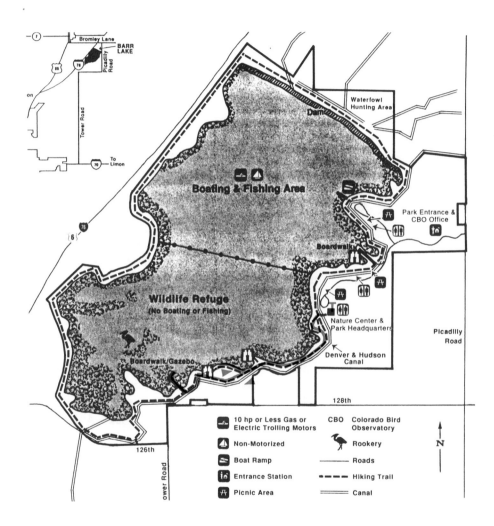

Map by Colorado State Parks

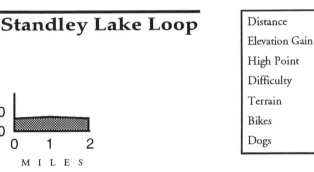

Distance	2.0 miles
Elevation Gain	50 ft
High Point	5,320 ft
Difficulty	●
Terrain	Trail
Bikes	Light
Dogs	Leashed

Trail Intro A quick inner-city hike above Lakewood's Standley Lake. There are several trails in the park, but the eastern ones are much nicer, free from the prairie dog infestation of the western trails. Bring a fishing rod; the lake shore is a popular casting spot.

Access from I-25 and 6th Ave. Drive west on 6th Ave. and then turn right (north) on Wadsworth. Drive north to 80th St. and turn left. At Kipling, turn right and continue to 86th parkway. Turn left on 86th, continue for 1 mile to Simms St. and turn right into the parking lot (keep an eye out, the park entrance is not marked, is narrow and comes up quickly).
Drive Time 35 minutes

The Hike Walking from the parking lot toward the lake, a Jeffco Open Space sign points to the trail junction. Turn right and walk along the upper trail, parallel, but well below, 86th Parkway. Intersect an unused road and a second trail, but continue straight along the main trail. Pass another trail and follow the main trail as it turns left and heads toward the lake. A short spur on your right leads to a good fishing spot. For the main route, parallel the lake, staying on the main trail as it leads back to the parking lot.

Trail Running Not really worth the time unless you're nearby. The western loop is mined with ankle twisting prairie dog holes so you only have a single 2.1 mile lap to trace.

With Kids A nice spot, especially being right in the city, but the prairie dogs and their burrows make me a little nervous with kids around.

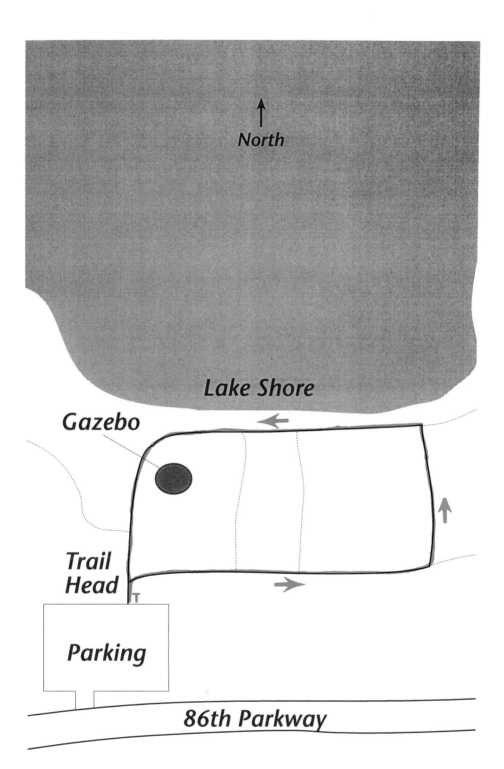

North

Lake Shore

Gazebo

Trail
Head

Parking

86th Parkway

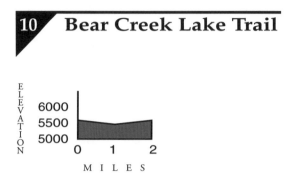

Distance	1.1 miles
Elevation Gain	50 ft
High Point	5,465 ft
Difficulty	●
Terrain	Trail
Bikes	Light
Dogs	Leashed

Trail Intro A shady creekside loop through the riparian habitat and tall cottonwoods spawned by Bear Creek. This route can be easily combined with all or a portion of the Bear Creek Lake – Game Field Trail (#5) for a longer walk.

Access from I-25 and 6th Ave. Drive west on 6th Ave. to Kipling. Turn south, go 4.4 miles to Morrison Road/Hwy. 8 and turn right (west). In 3.7 miles, turn left into Bear Creek Lake Park. Immediately turn left again, drive past the entrance gate, bear left at the stop sign and park in the first lot you come to.
Drive Time 25 minutes

The Hike Walk toward the creek and turn left on the horse trail. At the first fork, bear right, away from the horse trail, toward the creek. Walk under the power lines and cross the creek on a bridge. Turn right and upstream. Intersect a paved road and turn right on the path that parallels its right side. As you bend right, turn right onto a horse trail which descends briefly, but steeply. Come parallel to the stream and continue back to the start.

Trail Running A good run when combined with the Bear Creek Lake – Game Field Trail (#5) to make a 4.1 mile "figure 8" loop.

With Kids An ideal family stroll on a little-used, shady trail through the woods, along the banks of a stream.

Trail Notes It costs $3 to enter Bear Creek Lake Park.

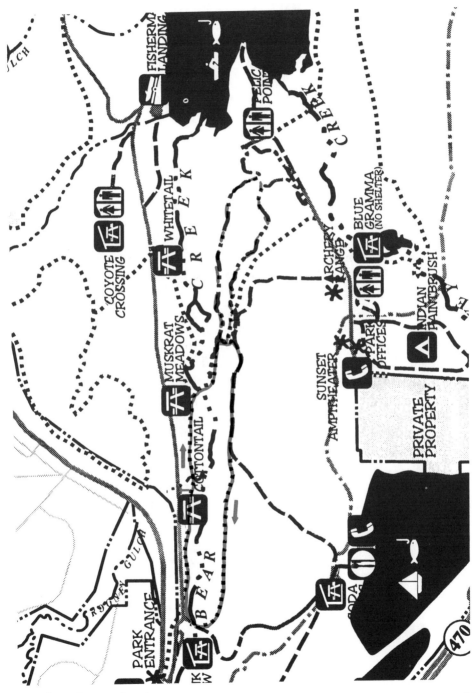

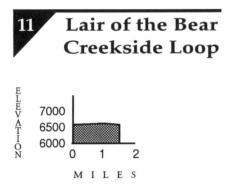

11 Lair of the Bear
Creekside Loop

Distance	1.5 miles
Elevation Gain	50 ft
High Point	6,550 ft
Difficulty	●
Terrain	Trail
Bikes	Light
Dogs	Leashed

Trail Intro A super stroll along the shady, cool banks of Bear Creek on mostly hiking-only trails.

Access from I-25 and 6th Ave. Drive west on 6th Ave. to Kipling. Turn south and continue 4.4 miles to Morrison Road/Hwy. 8. Turn right (west), drive through Morrison and bear right on Hwy. 74 toward Evergreen and Kitteridge. In 4.5 miles, look for Lair of the Bear Park on your left.
Drive Time 35 minutes

The Hike Beginning on the Brittlefern Trail, hike out along the Creekside Loop, paralleling Bear Creek. On the way back from the loop, take your second right on the hikers-only Creekside Trail. This trail follows the bank of Bear Creek. There are several spots where you can sit overlooking the creek and there are many picnic benches along the way. Follow the Creekside Trail to its intersection with the Bruin Bluff Trail at a bridge. Turn left on the Bruin Bluff, then left again onto the Creekside Trail and follow it back to the parking lot.

Trail Runners Do this run in combination with the Lair of the Bear – Bruin Bluff Trail (#12) for a 3.1 mile double loop with a single, short climb and descent, and shady cruising for the rest of the way.

With Kids An excellent family walk along mostly hikers-only trails (few bikers come to the park anyway since much of it is closed to them).

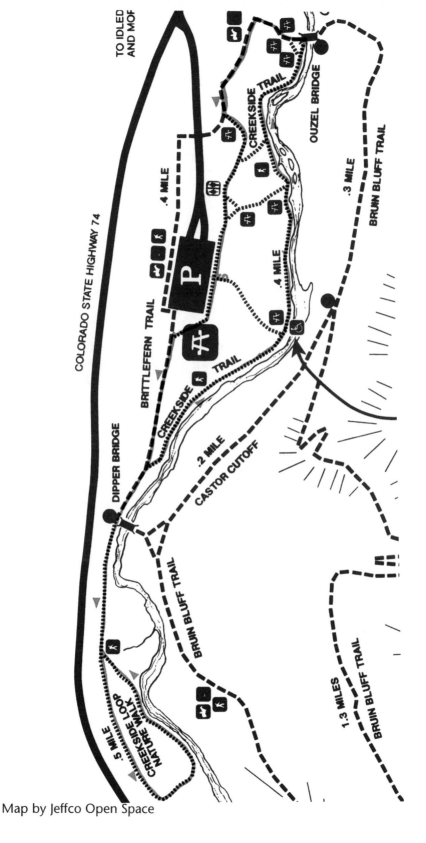

TO IDLED AND MOF

COLORADO STATE HIGHWAY 74

CREEKSIDE TRAIL

OUZEL BRIDGE

.4 MILE

BRITTLEFERN TRAIL

P

BRUIN BLUFF TRAIL

.3 MILE

.4 MILE

CREEKSIDE TRAIL

DIPPER BRIDGE

.2 MILE

CASTOR CUTOFF

BRUIN BLUFF TRAIL

.5 MILE

CREEKSIDE WALK NATURE

1.3 MILES

BRUIN BLUFF TRAIL

Map by Jeffco Open Space

31

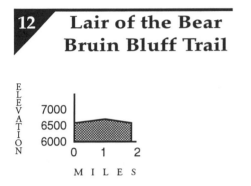

Distance	1.8 miles
Elevation Gain	125 ft
High Point	6,690 ft
Difficulty	●
Terrain	Trail
Bikes	Light
Dogs	Leashed

Trail Intro An easy loop which follows Bear Creek, climbs to a high point with views of the Bear Creek Canyon and then gradually descends back to the creek and the start.

Access from I-25 and 6th Ave. Drive west on 6th to Kipling, turn south and continue 4.4 miles to Morrison Road/Hwy. 8. Turn right (west), drive through Morrison and bear right on Hwy. 74 toward Evergreen and Kitteridge. In 4.5 miles, look for Lair of the Bear Park on your left.
Drive Time 30-35 minutes

The Hike Begin by following the Brittlefern Trail. Stay straight at the Creekside Trail and take your next left onto the Bruin Bluff Trail. Gradually ascend to a high point and then descend to a junction with the Brittlefern Trail. Turn onto the Brittlefern, cross Bear Creek, turn left on the Creekside Trail and follow it back to the start.

Trail Runners Run this in combination with the Lair of the Bear – Creekside Loop (#11) for a 3.1 mile double loop with a single, short climb and descent and shady cruising for the rest of the way.

With Kids The last time I was on this trail, a group of elementary school students were walking the loop with their science teacher. A nice family walk with few bikers or other faster movers.

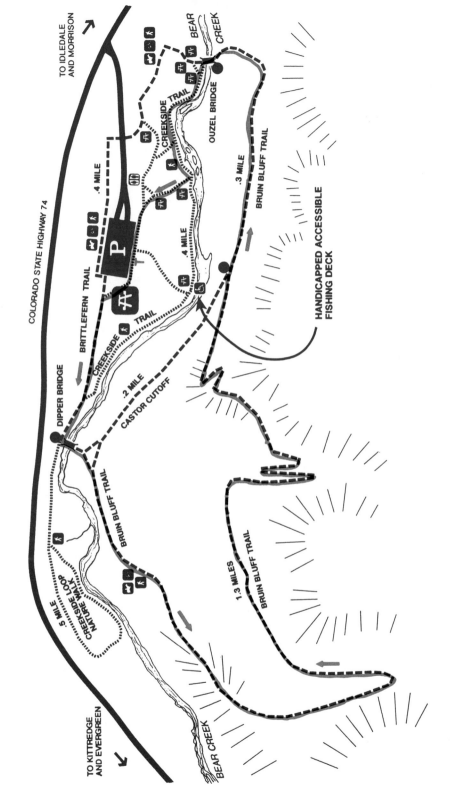

COLORADO STATE HIGHWAY 74

TO IDLEDALE AND MORRISON

TO KITTREDGE AND EVERGREEN

BEAR CREEK

BEAR CREEK

OUZEL BRIDGE

DIPPER BRIDGE

CREEKSIDE TRAIL

BRITTLEFERN TRAIL

CREEKSIDE TRAIL

BRUIN BLUFF TRAIL

BRUIN BLUFF TRAIL

BRUIN BLUFF TRAIL

CASTOR CUTOFF

CREEKSIDE LOOP NATURE WALK

HANDICAPPED ACCESSIBLE FISHING DECK

P

.4 MILE

.4 MILE

.2 MILE

.3 MILE

1.3 MILES

.5 MILE

Map by Jeffco Open Space

33

13 Mt. Sanitas Valley Trail

Distance	2.1 miles
Elevation Gain	400 ft
High Point	5,900 ft
Difficulty	●
Terrain	Trail
Bikes	No
Dogs	Leashed

Trail Intro An relatively easy, popular hike across the base of Mt. Sanitas. Expect to see lots of dogs, hikers, children and runners.

Access from I-25 and 6th Ave. Drive north on I-25 and turn west on U.S. Hwy. 36 (the Boulder Turnpike). Follow Hwy. 36 all the way into Boulder where it becomes 28th Street. At Canyon, turn left and follow it to 9th Street. Turn right on 9th and then left on Mapleton (at the top of the hill beyond Pearl St.). Follow Mapleton to the Mt. Sanitas Trailhead, which is just beyond the hospital, on the right.
Drive Time 45 minutes

The Hike From the parking area, walk up the stairs and join the road-width Valley Trail. About 200 yards up the trail, a singletrack trail branches off to the right. Turn right here, walk down to a stream and then climb for about 100 feet to another junction. Turn left here on the Dakota Ridge Trail. Bear right at every intersection as the Dakota Ridge Trail climbs one short, steep hill, then gradually ascends, above and parallel to the Valley Trail. The Dakota Trail ends where it reintersects the Valley Trail. Turn left here and walk down the Valley Trail back to the start.

Trail Running A short run with a hard climb to the end of the valley. For hard-cores in great shape, try the staircase-steep Mt. Sanitas Loop (it is the singletrack that branches off the start of the Valley Trail (there is a message board with a map of the area)).

With Kids This is a terrific, popular hike on a gradually ascending, road-width trail for folks with younger kids.

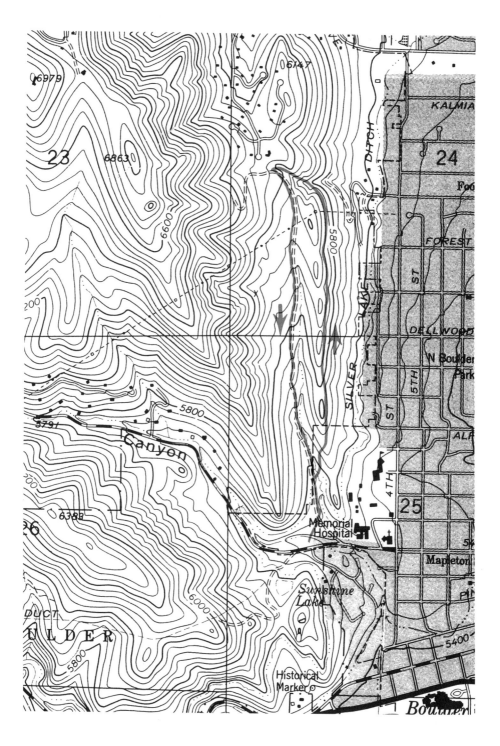

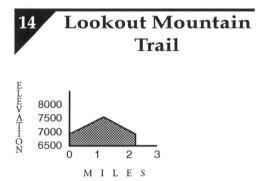

14	Lookout Mountain Trail	Distance	2.2 miles
		Elevation Gain	660 ft
		High Point	7,560 ft
		Difficulty	●
		Terrain	Trail
		Bikes	Light
		Dogs	Leashed

Trail Intro A soft, mostly smooth and gradually ascending trail with some of my favorite views of the Front Range. On a clear day, you can see Boulder's Flatirons 20 miles north.

Access from I-25 and 6th Ave. Drive 11.7 miles west on 6th Ave. to 19th Street, above Golden (the first light after the Jefferson County Government center). Turn left on 19th. In .3 miles, where you pass through two tall stone columns, 19th becomes Lookout Mountain Road. Continue 3 miles from the columns until you see a parking pull-off on your right and a sign for the Beaver Brook Trail. Park here.
Drive Time 25-30 minutes

The Hike The first .2 miles of the Lookout Mountain Trail is shared with the Beaver Brook Trail. At the first junction, bear left and uphill, following the sign for the Lookout Mountain Nature Center. Take your time strolling up so you don't miss any of the panoramic viewpoints. From the top, return as you came.

Trail Runners A short hill climb on a soft trail. There is a 1.3 mile nature loop trail (which I've never been on) at the top of the Lookout Mountain Trail which you could add to the run to make a longer circuit.

With Kids Generally light traffic and a short distance make it a good hike for a family. Its steep grade might be hard on little legs, however.

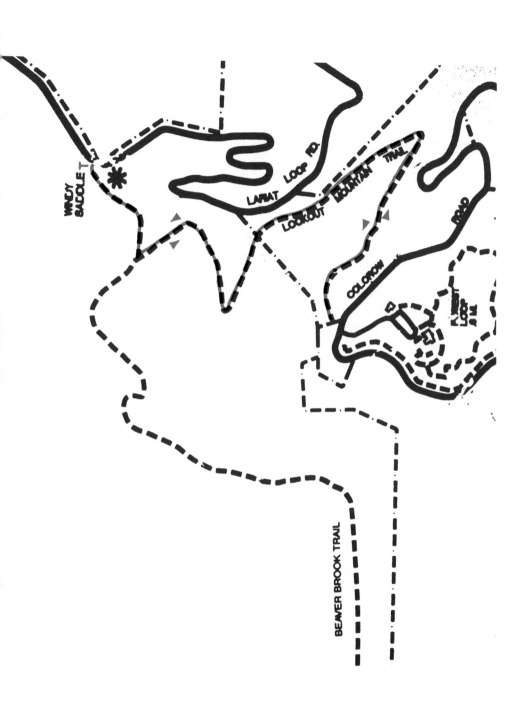

WINDY
SADDLE T

LARIAT LOOP RD.

LOOKOUT MOUNTAIN TRAIL

ROAD

COLOROW TRAIL

LOOP TRAIL

BEAVER BROOK TRAIL

Map by Jeffco Open Space

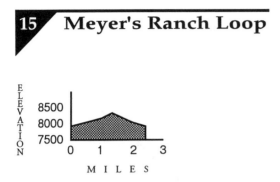

Distance	2.4 miles
Elevation Gain	465 ft
High Point	8,340 ft
Difficulty	●
Terrain	Trail
Bikes	Moderate
Dogs	Leashed

Trail Intro An often popular hike in the southern foothills on wide, smooth trails. By adding the Old Ski Run Trail, you can increase the distance to 4.5 miles and add 450 feet to the ascent.

Access Drive .5 miles west on I-70, turn south on C-470 and continue 5.6 miles to Hwy. 285. Turn south on Hwy. 285 and continue 12 miles to the Meyer's Ranch turn-off, marked with a brown Open Space sign on the left side of Hwy. 285.
Drive Time 40 minutes

The Hike Begin a counterclockwise loop of the park, turning right at every junction until you reach the Old Ski Run Trail. Continue past it, remaining on the Sunny Aspen Trail. Bear right on the Lodge Pole Loop at the next junction. Join the Owl's Perch Trail and follow it back to the start.

Trail Running A non-technical run on wide, smooth trails with gradually ascending hills. You can do up to 4.5 miles with 900 feet of climbing by tacking the Old Ski Run Trail onto the top of the Sunny Aspen Trail making a super length and toughness of run for those used to that distance and amount of ascending.

With Kids An easy walk that can be made as short or as long as you like. Doing just the Lodge Pole Loop is 1.9 miles with a 300 foot elevation gain, while the Sunny Aspen Trail makes a 2.4 mile stroll with an ascent of 475 feet. This trail is popular; expect to encounter other hikers, bikers and horseback riders.

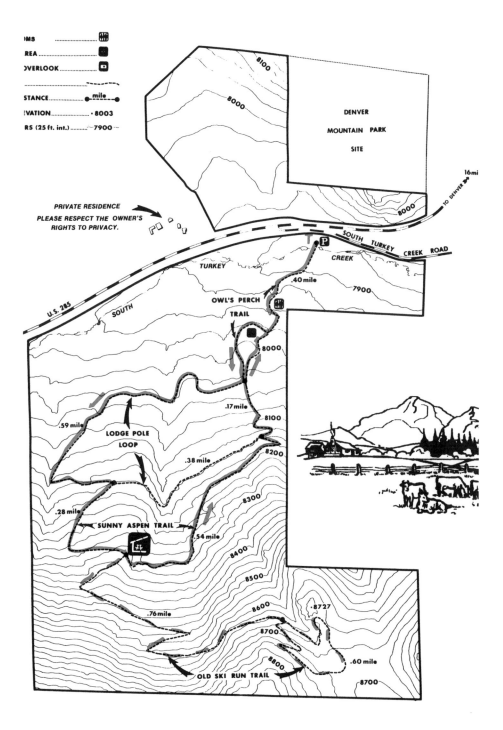

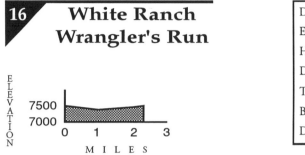

Distance	2.3 miles
Elevation Gain	165 ft
High Point	7,500 ft
Difficulty	●
Terrain	Trail
Bikes	Moderate
Dogs	Leashed

Trail Intro This short, placid loop travels the length of a green and wild-flower-rich stream valley on the north end of the park. There is one slightly steep ascent and descent but it is basically doable by anyone in moderately good shape and accustomed to the altitude.

Access from I-25 and 6th Ave. Drive 12.7 miles west on 6th Ave. to its intersection with Hwys. 6 & 93. Bear right on 93 and continue 1.4 miles to a 'White Ranch 10 Miles' sign and turn left on Golden Gate Canyon Rd., following the signs to White Ranch Park. In 2.8 miles, turn right on Crawford Gulch Road. In 3.8 more miles, turn right on Belcher Hill Road, continue 1.8 miles, through the park entrance, to the 2nd parking lot.
Drive Time 40 minutes

The Hike Walk down the road-width Rawhide Trail and then climb briefly to an intersection with the Wrangler's Run Trail. Turn right and downhill and walk through this little stream valley. At a second junction with the Rawhide Trail, turn right and ascend steeply. Continue past the Longhorn Trail and walk back back to the trailhead.

Trail Runners This is not my favorite run in the park; it starts with a downhill and ends with a climb. Instead, try White Ranch – Belcher Hill Trail (#17).

With Kids This is one of the better family routes in a hilly park; it is not too long, nor does it have much elevation change. If this still seems too hard, try an out-and-back along the very gentle Sawmill Trail instead; it starts from the second parking lot as well.

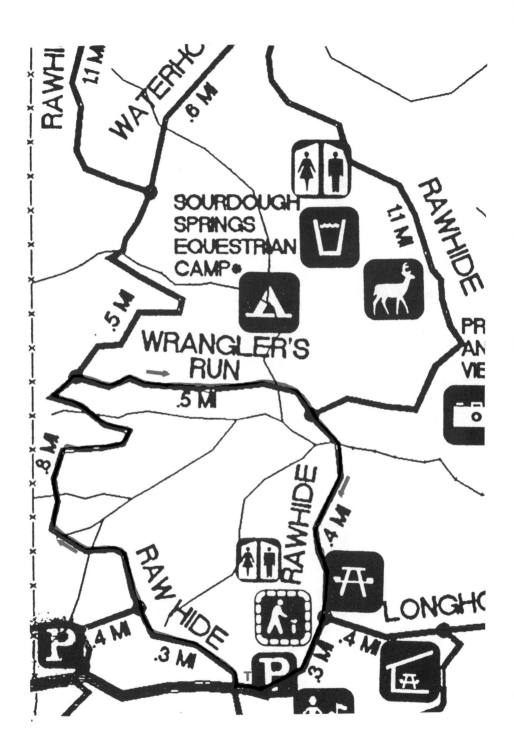

17 **White Ranch**
Belcher Hill Trail

Distance	2.6 miles
Elevation Gain	375 ft
High Point	7,800 ft
Difficulty	●
Terrain	Trail
Bikes	Moderate
Dogs	Leashed

Trail Intro A shorter hike through the more mountainous southwest end of the park, with views of the plains and mountains to the east and west, shady forests and broad meadows.

Access from I-25 and 6th Ave. Drive 12.7 miles west on 6th Ave. to its intersection with Hwys. 6 & 93. Bear right on 93 and continue 1.4 miles to a "White Ranch 10 Miles" sign and turn left onto Golden Gate Canyon Rd., following the signs for White Ranch Park. In 2.8 miles, turn right on Crawford Gulch Road. After 3.8 more miles, turn right on Belcher Hill Trail Road, continue 1.4 miles to the park entrance and park in the first lot **Drive Time** 40 minutes

The Hike Hike up the steep Mustang Trail and, at the first junction, turn left onto the Belcher Hill Trail. Crest and then descend along this somewhat steep trail, with its views to the east. At the Sawmill Trail, turn left and traverse a meadow to a lower parking lot. Cross the lot and join the road-width Rawhide Trail. Turn left at the Mustang Trail and walk back to the start.

Trail Runners This run begins with a tough climb on a steep, tree-lined single-track. Watch for bikers coming down. A long meadow descent is followed with a brief, hard climb back to the start/finish. As you can see from the map, you can easily add miles in every direction.

With Kids This hike is a little steep for kids. Instead, you might try White Ranch – Wrangler's Run (#16).

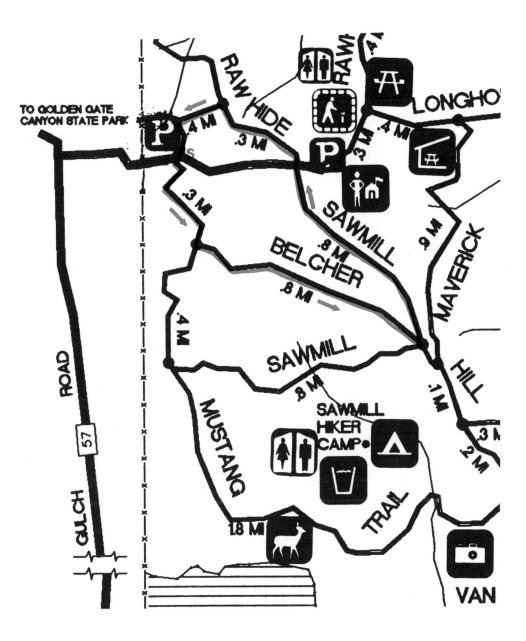

TO GOLDEN GATE
CANYON STATE PARK

RAW HIDE

RAW

LONGHO

.4 M

.3 M

.3 M

.4 M

.4 M

SAWMILL

.8 M

BELCHER

.8 M

.3 M

.4 M

SAWMILL

.9 M

MAVERICK

HILL

.1 M

.3 M

.2 M

.8 M

SAWMILL
HIKER
CAMP

MUSTANG

1.8 M

TRAIL

VAN

ROAD

57

GULCH

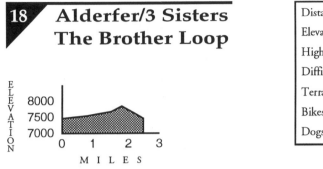

18	Alderfer/3 Sisters The Brother Loop

Distance	2.5 miles
Elevation Gain	320 ft
High Point	7,800 ft
Difficulty	●
Terrain	Trail
Bikes	Moderate
Dogs	Leashed

Trail Intro A moderately easy hike covering the most scenic areas of the park.

Access from I-25 and 6th Ave. Drive west on 6th Ave. and turn west on I-70. Exit at Evergreen Parkway (Exit #252). Turn left onto Hwy. 74 and follow it for 8.4 miles, past Bergen Park, until it intersects Hwy. 73 in the town of Evergreen. Turn right on Hwy. 73. In .7 miles, turn right on Buffalo Park Rd. Continue 1.5 miles to the Alderfer/Three Sisters east parking lot (the first one you come to).
Drive Time 45 minutes

The Hike From the parking lot, turn right on the Hidden Fawn Trail and follow it to its intersection with the Three Sisters Trail. Turn right on the Sisters Trail and walk through this interesting rock formation. At the next junction, turn left and then left again onto the Brother Trail. At the top of the Brother are flat rocks to sit on and enjoy 360° views of the surrounding mountains and the town of Evergreen and Evergreen Lake. Retrace your steps down the Brother and turn left on the Ponderosa Trail. At the next junction, turn right and walk back to the start.

Trail Running A short run with a good warm up and some nice, though brief hill climbs. With so many other trails in the park you can easily add more distance (or check out the 3 Sister Loop (#27)). The only downside is the great popularity of the park.

With Kids There are a few, short steep sections, but otherwise it's a nice walk that is probably not too long for most active children.

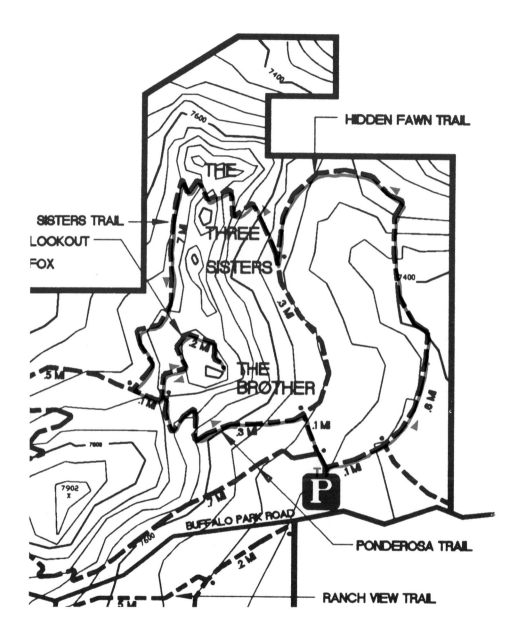

HIDDEN FAWN TRAIL

THE
THREE
SISTERS

SISTERS TRAIL
LOOKOUT
FOX

7400

7600

7400

.3 M

.2 M

THE
BROTHER

.5 M

.1 M

.6 M

.3 M

.1 M

.1 M

7902
X

7800

.1 M

P

.2 M

PONDEROSA TRAIL

BUFFALO PARK ROAD

7600

.2 M

RANCH VIEW TRAIL

.5 M

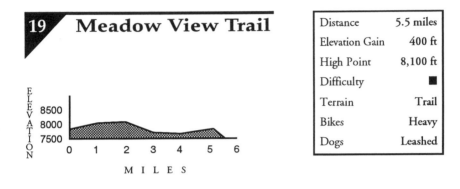

Distance	5.5 miles
Elevation Gain	400 ft
High Point	8,100 ft
Difficulty	■
Terrain	Trail
Bikes	Heavy
Dogs	Leashed

Trail Intro A longer walk across open meadows at the foot of Bergen Peak. Great in spring and fall, but can be hot in summer. Lots of wildflowers in season.

Access from I-25 and 6th Ave. Drive west on 6th Ave. and turn west on I-70. Exit at Evergreen Parkway (Exit #252). Drive past Bergen Park. 1.7 miles past Squaw Pass Road (the Mt. Evans Road), turn right on Lewis Ridge Road at a traffic light; the park is marked with a brown Elk Meadow Park sign.
Drive Time 35 minutes

The Hike Begin on the Meadow View Trail. At the first junction, turn right on the Sleepy S Trail. Continue past a junction with the Elkridge Trail and turn left on the Painter's Pause Trail which parallels Hwy. 74, but is generally out-of-sight on it. At the end of the Painter's Pause Trail, turn left on the Meadow View Trail and ascend for 1 mile to a junction with the Too Long Trail. Go left on the Meadow View Trail and climb and descend along this rolling path until you intersect the Elkridge Trail. Continue straight along the Meadow View Trail past the Bergen Peak Trail and return to the start.

Trail Running A smooth, rolling singletrack through the meadows; great fun! For seasoned experts, try the long "tester" run: the big outside loop to the top of Bergen Peak (10.7 miles and 2,000 feet of climbing!).

With Kids This trail is pretty long for younger kids and can be very hot in summer. In the vicinity, try part of one of the Alderfer/3 Sisters Trails (#18, #27 or #34) instead.

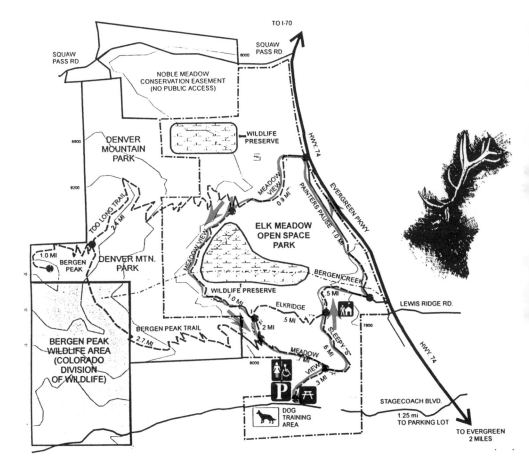

TO I-70

SQUAW PASS RD.

SQUAW PASS RD.

NOBLE MEADOW CONSERVATION EASEMENT (NO PUBLIC ACCESS)

WILDLIFE PRESERVE

DENVER MOUNTAIN PARK

8800

9200

TOO LONG TRAIL 2.4 MI

MEADOW VIEW .9 MI

ELK MEADOW OPEN SPACE PARK

PAINTERS PAUSE 1.0 MI

HWY 74

EVERGREEN PKWY

1.0 MI

BERGEN PEAK

DENVER MTN. PARK

MEADOW VIEW

BERGEN CREEK

WILDLIFE PRESERVE 1.0 MI

ELKRIDGE .5 MI

.5 MI

LEWIS RIDGE RD.

BERGEN PEAK WILDLIFE AREA (COLORADO DIVISION OF WILDLIFE)

BERGEN PEAK TRAIL 2.7 MI

2 MI

SLEEPY S .6 MI

7600

HWY 74

8000

MEADOW VIEW .7 MI

P

MEADOW VIEW .3 MI

DOG TRAINING AREA

STAGECOACH BLVD.

1.25 mi TO PARKING LOT

TO EVERGREEN 2 MILES

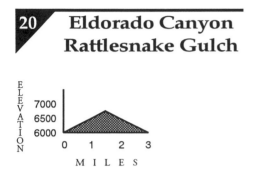

20 Eldorado Canyon
Rattlesnake Gulch

Distance	3.0 miles
Elevation Gain	750 ft
High Point	6,750 ft
Difficulty	■
Terrain	Trail
Bikes	Light
Dogs	Leashed

Trail Intro An easy trail to the ruins of Crags Hotel, a retreat for Denver's rich at the beginning of the century. The highlight of the trail is the views of spectacular Eldorado Canyon where you can watch world-calls climbers scaling the walls of this famed climbing mecca.

Access from I-25 and 6th Ave. Drive west on 6th Ave. to its intersection with Hwys. 6 & 93. Bear right on 93 and follow it for 14.6 miles to Colorado State Highway 170/Eldorado Canyon State Park (there is a traffic light here). Turn left and drive to the end of the road where it enters the Park. Continue .5 miles past the park entrance to the Rattlesnake Gulch parking lot.
Drive Time 45 minutes

The Hike Begin walking up the road-width Rattlesnake Gulch Trail which heads uphill and back toward the park entrance from the parking lot. Switchback past the Fowler Trail and continue uphill. Views of the canyon emerge as you ascend.

Trail Running A nice out-and-back hill climb on a smooth trail with great canyon views.

With Kids A perfect family hike. It is not too long, but it can be hot in summer as it does not have much shade.

Trail Notes It costs $4 to enter Eldorado State Park.

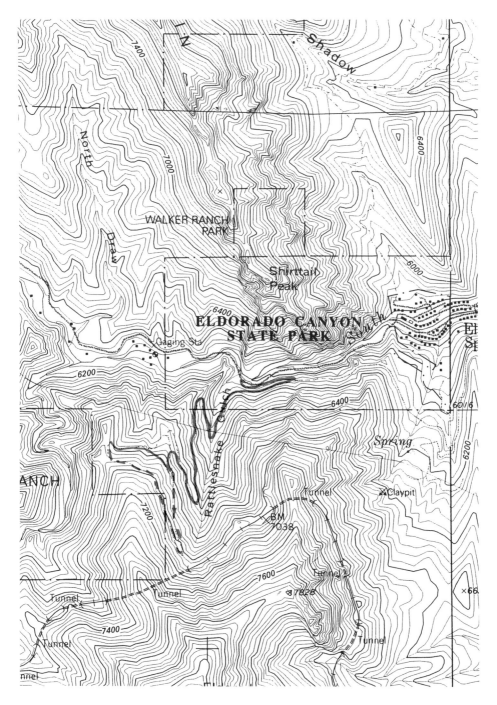

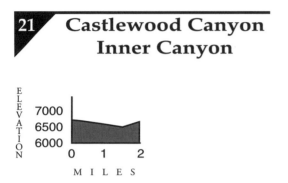

Castlewood Canyon
Inner Canyon

Distance	2 miles
Elevation Gain	200 ft
High Point	6,500 ft
Difficulty	■
Terrain	Trail
Bikes	No
Dogs	Leashed

Trail Intro A short loop through the most dramatic parts of Castlewood Canyon. For a nice side trip, walk about .25 miles downstream to the Castlewood Canyon dam ruins. (The dam broke in 1933 and flooded Denver, 15 miles downstream. The damage is pictured on pages 52-53 and 84-85.)

Access from I-25 and 6th Ave. Drive south on I-25. Take the second Castle Rock Exit (#182), following the signs for Hwy. 86 and Franktown. Cross over the highway and take your first right into Castle Rock. Turn left at 5th Ave. onto Hwy. 86, again following the signs for Franktown. When you reach Franktown, turn right on Hwy. 83, drive 5 miles and turn right into Castlewood Canyon State Park, which is clearly signed.
Drive Time 45-50 minutes

The Hike Begin by switchbacking down the Inner Canyon Trail to Cherry Creek. At the junction with the Lake Gulch Trail, you can walk downstream to the dam ruins or continue along the Lake Gulch Trail which gradually ascends through scrub desert back to the parking lot, offering nice views to the west along the way.

Trail Running A very short run. Watch for the ankle twisting rocks along the Lake Gulch ascent. For a longer run, tack on a side trip to the dam and then climb onto the Rim Rock Trail and continue for as long as you'd like (an extra 3.3+ miles for the whole lower loop with the Creek Bottom Trail. Read the description for the Rim Rock Trail (#36) for details).

With Kids An pretty ideal family hike in spring or fall down to the rocks on the banks of Cherry Creek. It might be too hot in summer, call the visitor's center and check first (303-668-5242).

Trail Notes It costs $5 to enter Castlewood Canyon State Park.

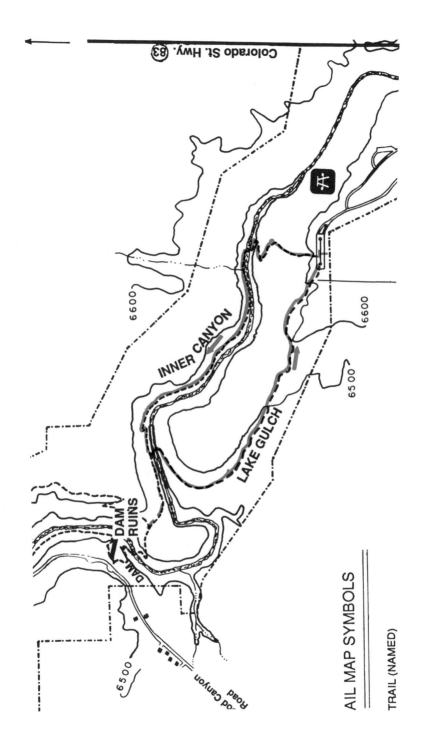

Colorado St. Hwy. (83)

6600

INNER CANYON

6600

6500

LAKE GULCH

DAM RUINS

DAM

6500

...od Canyon
Road

AIL MAP SYMBOLS

TRAIL (NAMED)

The Castlewood Canyon Dam.

The remains of the Castlewood Canyon Dam after it broke in 1933.

Photo © Denver Public Library - Western History Department

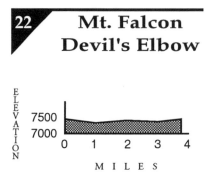

Distance	3.8 miles
Elevation Gain	220 ft
High Point	7,465 ft
Difficulty	■
Terrain	Trail
Bikes	Heavy
Dogs	Leashed

Trail Intro The Devil's Elbow Trail crosses wildflower-covered meadows and climbs to a high viewpoint overlooking Denver. The backside of the loop passes one of my favorite spots, the Eagle's Eye Shelter, with its commanding views of the hills and peaks of the Front Range.

Access from 6th Ave. and I-70 Drive .5 miles west on I-70 and turn south on C-470. Turn south again on Hwy. 285. Drive 4.2 miles up Turkey Creek Canyon and turn right on Parmalee Road, marked with a brown sign for Mt. Falcon. Drive up Parmalee Road, following the signs for the park, which is clearly marked.
Drive Time 30 minutes

The Hike Begin on the road-width Castle Trail. Pass the Parmalee and Meadow Trails but stay on the Castle Trail. In .8 miles, the Walker Home Ruins are on the left. Turn right on the Meadow Trail and descend to a junction with the Old Ute Trail. Turn left and hike up the Old Ute Trail, staying right at a fork. At a second fork, turn onto the Devil's Elbow Trail and do a clockwise loop. At the top is the aforementioned viewpoint. Back at the Old Ute Trail, turn right and walk to its end. Continue past the Meadow and Parmalee Trails and turn left on the Tower Trail. Hike up to and past the fire lookout tower and descend to the Eagle's Eye Shelter. Rejoin the Meadow Trail at the bottom of the Tower Trail, walk back to the Castle Trail, turn left and return to the start.

Trail Running An easy 5K on smooth paths with minimal elevation gain. Also makes a challenging longer run when combined with the Parmalee (#25) or Castle (#26) Trails.

With Kids Pretty long for kids. Try the Tower Trail (#7) instead.

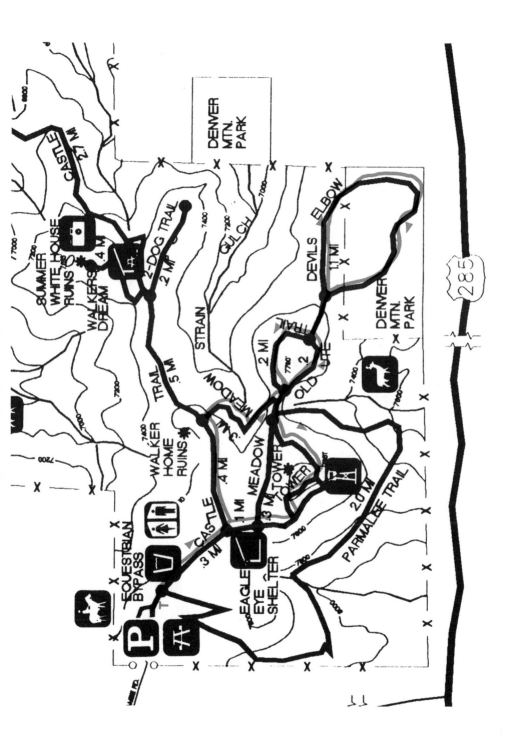

Distance	3.5 miles
Elevation Gain	550 ft
High Point	6,550 ft
Difficulty	■
Terrain	Trail
Bikes	Light
Dogs	Leashed

Trail Intro Another favorite trail with its variations in terrain and scenery (from high desert to low forest, and from Denver back into the foothills), plus the added bonus of the Meadowlark Trail segment of the loop being open to hikers only.

Access from I-25 and 6th Ave. Drive west on 6th Ave. to Kipling and turn south. Drive to the end of Kipling, just past C-470 and follow it as it bends around to the right and becomes Deer Creek Canyon Road. Follow the signs for Deer Creek Canyon Park to the trailhead; 3 miles.
Drive Time 30 minutes

The Hike Begin by hiking up the sandy and, at first, narrow Plymouth Creek Trail, through high desert red sandstone and cactus. At a junction, turn right onto the hikers-only Meadowlark Trail. Switchback up into increasingly dense foliage. Just beyond the top of the loop you'll get a peek into Deer Creek Canyon before gradually descending back into the plains to the start/finish.

Trail Running A great loop with a sustained but gradual up, followed by a fast descent. Not technical, but the first mile climb can be a sandy. The foot-traffic only back side is smooth and hardpacked. For a longer run, go to the top of the Plymouth Mountain Trail (5.4 miles 1,100 feet), another mostly hiking-only route.

With Kids Try an out-and-back on the hikers-only Meadowlark Trail; you can turn around at any point if anyone is pooped, and you don't have to worry about horse or bike traffic. The Meadowlark Trail is the most interesting part of The Hike to boot.

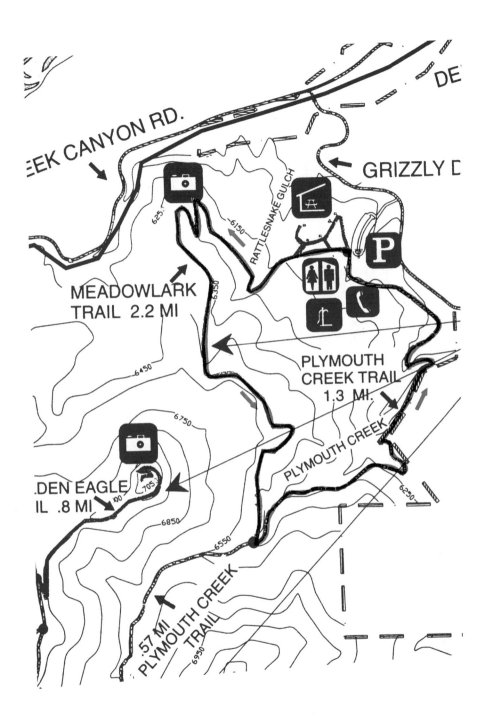

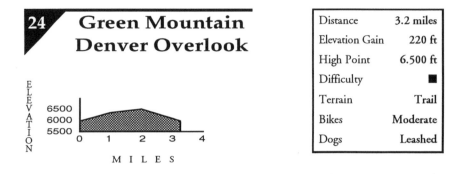

24	**Green Mountain**	Distance	3.2 miles
	Denver Overlook	Elevation Gain	220 ft
		High Point	6.500 ft
		Difficulty	■
		Terrain	Trail
		Bikes	Moderate
		Dogs	Leashed

Trail Intro A rocky, little loop on the eastern end of Green Mountain, with super views of Denver and Red Rocks. In summer, this is a prime wild-flower-viewing spot. The ascent is used by many bikers but the descent is little traveled.

Access from I-25 and 6th Ave. Drive west on 6th Ave. to the Simms/Union Exit. Turn left (south) on Union and drive to its end at Alameda. Turn right on Alameda. Drive 1.7 miles and turn right into the Green Mountain Parking Lot.
Drive Time 20 minutes

The Hike From the parking lot, walk south (left) on the steep trail leaving the parking lot by the entrance. Walk up and over the hump and turn right on the trail at the bottom of the other side. At a 3-way intersection, turn right and switchback uphill. At the next junction, bear left and walk through a little valley. Near the top of the climb, look for a side trail on your left leading to a Red Rocks/Front Range overlook. At the top of the main trail, intersect a road. Turn right on the road. Pass several trails but stay on the road to the radio tower. After the tower, stay straight at the first junction then turn right at the second onto a sharply descending, rocky trail. At a junction near the bottom of the trail, stay right on the less steep option and return to the start.

Trail Running This trail is too rocky to be a good run. If you are a fit runner, try the Lonesome Loop (#42) instead.

With Kids This trail is probably too rocky and steep for younger kids to walk, or for you to feel comfortable carrying them.

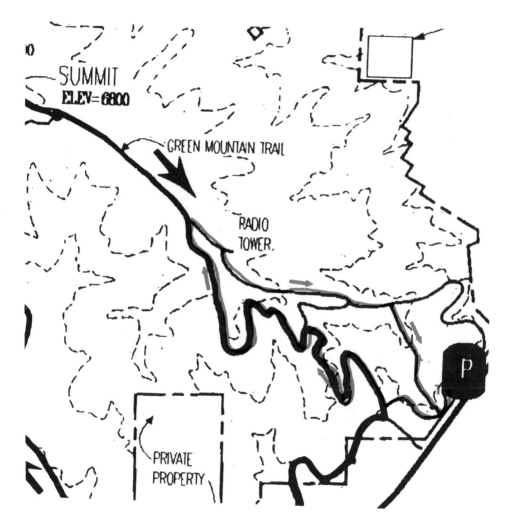

SUMMIT
ELEV= 6800

GREEN MOUNTAIN TRAIL

RADIO
TOWER.

P

PRIVATE
PROPERTY

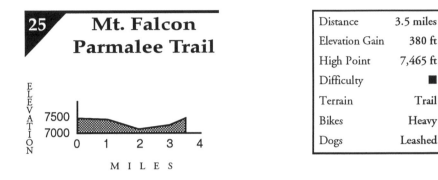

Distance	3.5 miles
Elevation Gain	380 ft
High Point	7,465 ft
Difficulty	■
Terrain	Trail
Bikes	Heavy
Dogs	Leashed

Trail Intro A longer hike across lush meadows and through cool forests on the southwest end of the park.

Access from 6th Ave. and I-70 Drive .5 miles west on I-70, turn south on C-470, and then turn south again on Hwy. 285. Drive 4.2 miles up Turkey Creek Canyon on 285 and turn right on Parmalee Road, marked with a brown sign for Mt. Falcon. Drive up Parmalee Road, following the signs for the park.
Drive Time 40 minutes

The Hike Start down the Castle Trail which is a road closed to motor vehicles. Pass the Parmalee and Meadow Trails and continue to the Walker Home Ruins. Turn right here onto the Meadow Trail. At its end, join the Parmalee Trail. Follow the Parmalee as it gradually ascends, descends and the ascends more steeply. The trail ends at the Castle Trail. Turn left and return to the trailhead.

Trail Running For its length, this is one of the best singletracks along the Front Range. This route has smooth trails with a lot of variety in terrain and elevation changes., as well as stellar scenery.

With Kids This trail may be a bit long for younger kids, but would be nice for older ones. Expect to see many bikers.

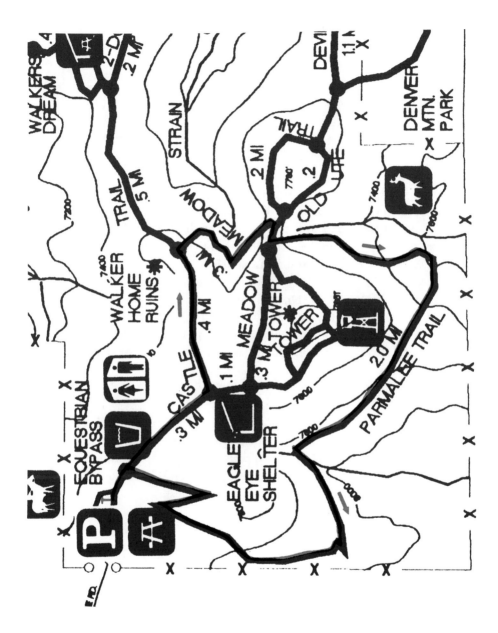

Map by Jeffco Open Space

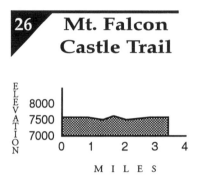

Distance	3.4 miles
Elevation Gain	250 ft
High Point	7,600 ft
Difficulty	■
Terrain	Trail
Bikes	Heavy
Dogs	Leashed

26 Mt. Falcon Castle Trail

Trail Intro Leads to the ruins of the never completed Summer White House. According to the Jeffco Open Space, the retreat was the idea of John Brisben Walker, a large land owner in the area at the turn of the century. Brisben started the project in the early 1900s but the dream ended with the start of W.W. I. The trail to the ruins was named in his honor.

Access from 6th Ave. and I-70 Drive .5 miles west on I-70, turn south on C-470, and then south again onto Hwy. 285. Drive 4.2 miles up Turkey Creek Canyon and turn right on Parmalee Road, marked with a brown sign for Mt. Falcon. Drive up Parmalee Road, following the signs for the park, which is clearly marked.
Drive Time 40 minutes

The Hike Start down the Castle Trail, a road closed to motor vehicles. At .7 miles, pass the ruins of Walker's home, which burned down in 1918. Another half-mile along is a shelter with picnic tables and the head of the Walker's Dream Trail. From the shelter, the Summer White House is a short, rocky and steep .4 mile walk. Return as you came.

Trail Running A long flat road-width trail followed by a steep, short, rocky climb. Try the Devil's Elbow (#22) or the Parmalee Trail (#25) instead.

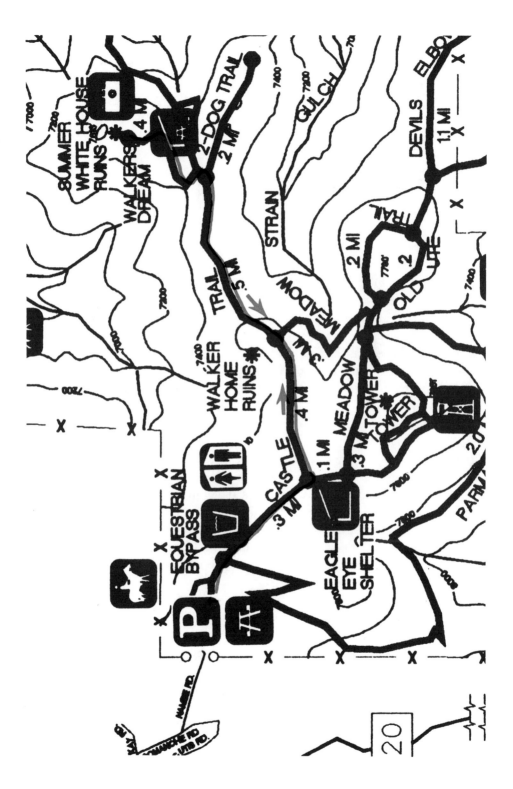

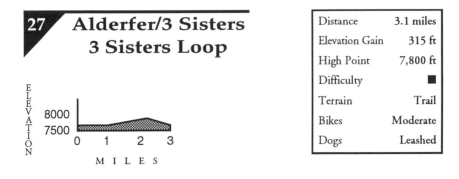

27 Alderfer/3 Sisters
3 Sisters Loop

Distance	3.1 miles
Elevation Gain	315 ft
High Point	7,800 ft
Difficulty	■
Terrain	Trail
Bikes	Moderate
Dogs	Leashed

Trail Intro A nice, though popular walk. Be sure to make the trip to the top of the Brother for fantastic views in all directions.

Access from I-25 and 6th Ave. Drive west on 6th Ave. and turn west on I-70. Exit at Evergreen Parkway (Exit #252). Turn left on Hwy. 74 and follow it for 8.4 miles, past Bergen Park, until it intersects Hwy. 73 in the town of Evergreen. Turn right on Hwy. 73. In .7 miles, turn right on Buffalo Park Road. Continue 2.3 miles to the Alderfer/Three Sisters west (the 2nd) parking lot.
Drive Time 45 minutes

The Hike Begin by hiking east on the Silver Fox Trail. Bear left at a junction with the Ponderosa Trail, staying on the Silver Fox. At the next junction, turn right and then intersect the Sisters Trail. Turn left and do a clockwise loop of the Sisters. Continue past the Hidden Fawn Trail and turn right on the Ponderosa Trail. Walk up and back on the Brother to the view point. Turn right at the bottom of the Brother and then bear left on the Ponderosa. Turn right onto the Silver Fox at the next junction and walk back to the start.

Trail Running An excellent run for any runner in good shape. Starts with a flat warm up then has two climbs, through the Sisters and the Brother, before a flat return to the start. Keep an eye out for bikers.

With Kids Perhaps a bit long. Try The Brother Loop (#18) instead.

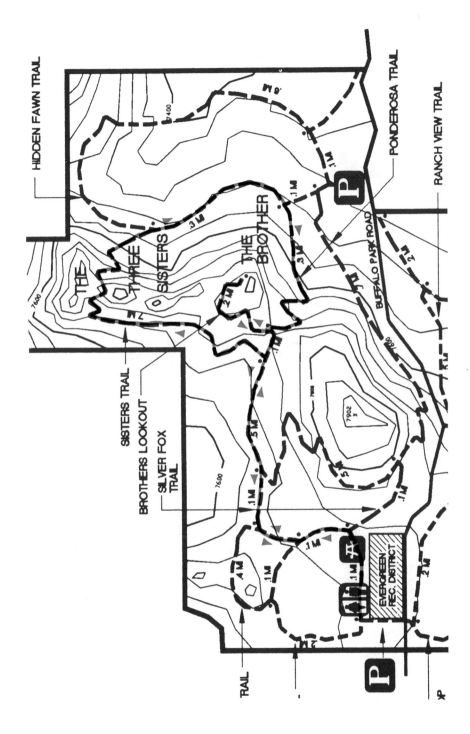

Map by Jeffco Open Space

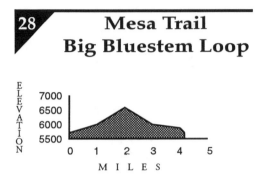

28	**Mesa Trail** **Big Bluestem Loop**	Distance	4.2 miles
		Elevation Gain	900 ft
		High Point	6,575 ft
		Difficulty	■
		Terrain	Trail
		Bikes	No
		Dogs	Leashed

ELEVATION

7000
6500
6000
5500

0 1 2 3 4 5

M I L E S

Trail Intro This is my favorite section of the Mesa Trail, with stunning views of the Flatirons and the Devil's Thumb rock formation.

Access from I-25 and 6th Ave. Drive west on 6th Ave. to its intersection with Hwys. 6 & 93. Bear right on 93 and follow it 14.6 miles to Colorado State Highway 170/Eldorado Canyon State Park (there is a traffic light here). Turn left, drive 1.7 miles, and turn right into the Mesa Trailhead parking lot.
Drive Time 40 minutes

The Hike Begin walking up the road-width Mesa Trail. Walk past junctions with a number of other trails, but remain on the Mesa Trail and gradually ascend. As you near the foothills, the trail ascends more steeply. Crest the top of the hill and descend briefly into a beautiful little valley. The Flatirons and the Devil's Thumb loom above. Pass the Shadow Canyon Trail and then turn right and downhill on the Big Bluestem Trail. Walk through wild flower carpeted meadows and pass the ruins of a old cabin. As you descend, you pass from the pine tree of the foothills into the yucca and cactus of the high desert on the edge of the Great Plains. At the bottom of the Big Bluestem Trail, turn right on a road-width trail toward the Mesa Trail, then turn left back on to the Mesa Trail and descend back to the start.

Trail Running A classic run with exceptional views and gradual climbing and descending. Add extra miles by continuing out-and-back along the Mesa Trail beyond its intersection with the Bluestem Trail.

With Kids A wonderful hike, though it may be a bit long for younger children. The trail can be quite hot in summer as it does not have much shade.

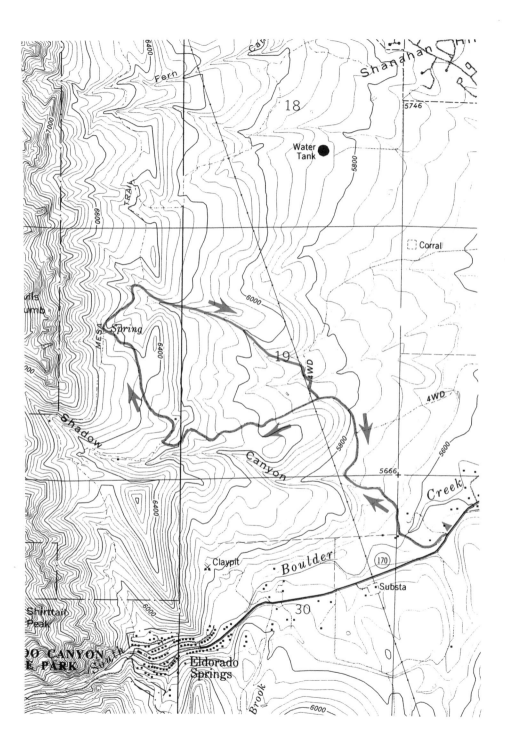

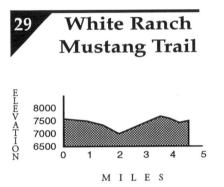

White Ranch Mustang Trail

Distance	4.5 miles
Elevation Gain	700 ft
High Point	7,650 ft
Difficulty	■
Terrain	Trail
Bikes	Moderate
Dogs	Leashed

Trail Intro This is a favorite, partly because it is one of the least used trails in the 3,000 acre White Ranch Park. The hike begins with a meadow crossing overlooking the plains and the city, including downtown Denver in the distance. The trail then descends into a canyon with mountain views, streams and a rare Front Range aspen stand. Numerous, very tame deer are a frequent sight.

Access from I-25 and 6th Ave. Drive 12.7 miles west on 6th Ave. to its intersection with Hwys. 6 & 93. Bear right on 93 and continue 1.4 miles to a "White Ranch 10 Miles" sign and turn left. Follow the signs to White Ranch Park: in 2.8 miles, turn right on Crawford Gulch Road. In 3.8 more miles, turn right on Belcher Hill Road and continue 1.4 miles to the park entrance. Park in the first lot you come to.
Drive Time 45 minutes

The Hike Walk down the Mustang Trail to its end. Turn right on the road-width Rawhide Trail and walk up to and across a parking lot, joining the Sawmill Trail on the other side of the road. The Sawmill Trail crosses a wide meadow then enters the woods. The Sawmill Trail ends at the Belcher Hill Trail. Turn left on the Belcher and walk to its intersection with the Mustang Trail. Turn right and walk downhill on this little used, lovely trail. Hike past the Sawmill Trail. At the top of the ascent, intersect the Belcher Hill Trail, but continue across it, following the Mustang back to the start.

Trail Running A great loop with many ups and downs, both short and sustained. Super views and many trees make this one of the better mid-summer and early fall options. It's one of the last trails in the park to dry out in spring and after storms, however.

With Kids This trail is too long for younger children.

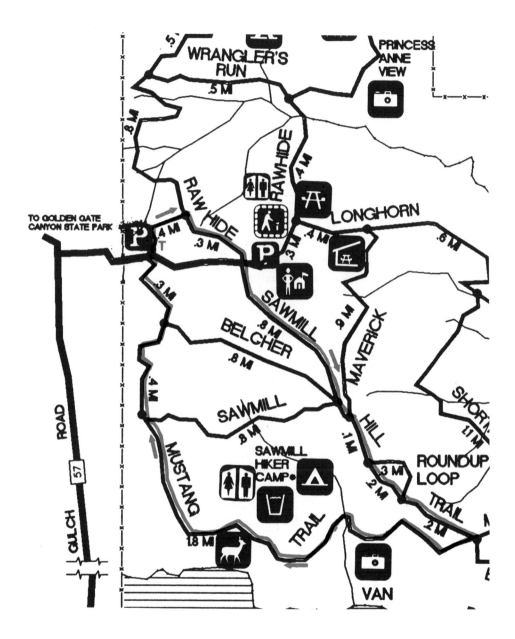

WRANGLER'S RUN

PRINCESS ANNE VIEW

.5

.5 M

.8 M

RAWHIDE

.4 M

RAW HIDE

.4 M

LONGHORN

.4 M

.3 M

.6 M

TO GOLDEN GATE CANYON STATE PARK

P

.4 M

.3 M

.3 M

SAWMILL

.8 M

MAVERICK

.3 M

.9 M

BELCHER

.8 M

.4 M

SAWMILL

.8 M

HILL

.1 M

SHORT

1.1 M

ROUNDUP LOOP

MUSTANG

SAWMILL HIKER CAMP

.3 M

.2 M

TRAIL

.2 M

ROAD

57

GULCH

1.8 M

TRAIL

VAN

Map by Jeffco Open Space

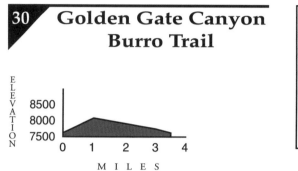

Distance	3.5 miles
Elevation Gain	520 ft
High Point	8,100 ft
Difficulty	■
Terrain	Trail/Road
Bikes	Light
Dogs	Leashed

Trail Intro A peaceful hike with Golden Gate Canyon views that travels through forests, among wildflowers and across a stream.

Access from I-25 and 6th Ave. Drive west on 6th Ave. to its intersection with Hwys. 6 & 93. Bear right on Hwy. 93, toward Boulder, and drive 1.4 miles to Golden Gate Canyon Road, marked with a brown sign for Golden Gate State Park and "White Ranch 10 Miles." Follow Golden Gate Canyon Road to the park entrance. Take your first right, toward the visitor's center, and continue 3.2 miles to the Ranch Ponds parking lot.
Drive Time 45-50 minutes

The Hike Hike up about 100 feet to a junction. Turn left and begin climbing steeply. At the next junction, 1.1 miles up, turn right on the Burro/Mountain Lion Trail. In .1 miles, turn right on the Burro Trail. In another .1 miles, stay right on the Burro Trail. Descend to a stream, cross a bridge and bear right. In .2 miles, the trail forks again. Stay left, hiking away from the maintenance barn. In .3 miles, intersect a dirt road and turn left onto it. In .6 miles, intersect the Mountain Lion Trail and turn right onto it. Bear left at the next junction and descend into a parking area. Cross the parking lot and rejoin the trail on the other side, turning right and following it back to the start.

Trail Running A tough run with many rocky sections and steep ascents and descents. Makes a good mid-summer route with its high altitude and largely shady terrain.

With Kids This is a fairly long hike with a steep climb that may not be suitable for younger children. Be sure older kids are up for it first.

Trail Notes It costs $5 to enter Golden Gate Canyon State Park.

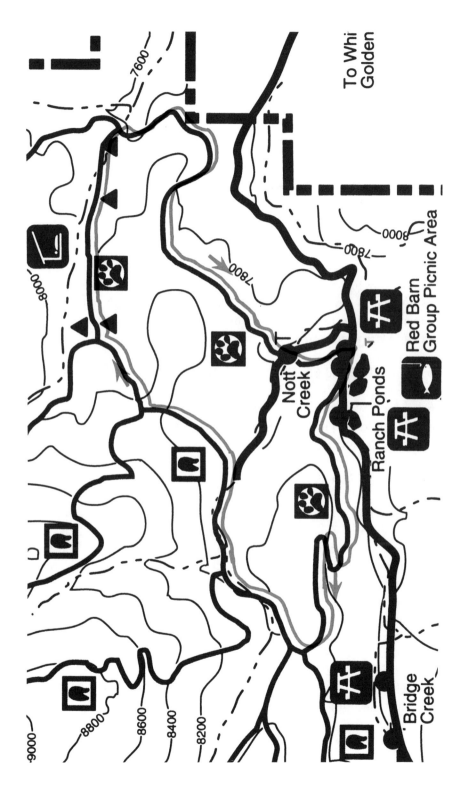

To Whi
Golden

Red Barn
Group Picnic Area

Ranch Ponds

Nott
Creek

Bridge
Creek

7600

8000

7800

8000

7800

8800

8600

8400

8200

9000

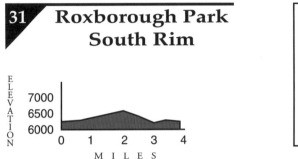

31 Roxborough Park South Rim

Distance	3.8 miles
Elevation Gain	375 ft
High Point	6,600 ft
Difficulty	■
Terrain	Trail
Bikes	No
Dogs	No

Trail Intro A longer tour of the south end of Roxborough Park. The hike begins by traveling through a jungle of scrub oak that seems poised to overgrow the trail at any moment. The trail then climbs to a high ridge offering a superb overview the park's red sandstone "flatirons" formations to the north and Carpenter Peak to the west.

Access from I-25 and 6th Ave. Drive west on 6th Ave. to Wadsworth, turn south and follow it under C-470. 5 miles past C-470, turn left on the Roxborough/Waterton Road. Bear left at the fork and continue on the Roxborough road to its end at Rampart Range Road. Turn right and follow the signs for another 4.4 miles to the Roxborough Park visitor's center parking lot.
Drive Time 45 minutes

The Hike From the visitor's center, join the South Rim Trail. Stay right at a turn-off for the Willow Trail, then bear left at the Carpenter Peak Trail junction and begin climbing to the ridge. After circling the rim of the park descend to another junction with the Willow Trail and turn left on it, crossing a meadow and meandering back to the visitor's center.

Trail Running A great, tough, though shorter, run with technical challenges, steep descents and super views. A long drive, but worth it for the serious runner! Can be hot in summer.

With Kids This is a pretty long route for children. Try Roxborough Park – Fountain Valley (#6) instead.

Trail Notes It costs $5 to enter Roxborough State Park.

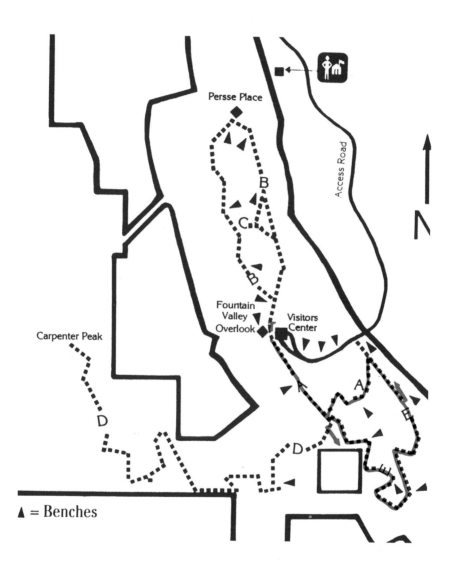

Persse Place

Access Road

B

C

B

Fountain
Valley
Overlook

Visitors
Center

Carpenter Peak

A

E

D

D

▲ = Benches

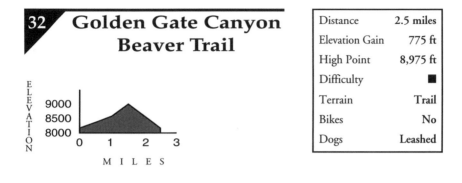

32 Golden Gate Canyon Beaver Trail

Distance	2.5 miles
Elevation Gain	775 ft
High Point	8,975 ft
Difficulty	■
Terrain	Trail
Bikes	No
Dogs	Leashed

Trail Intro A soft, pine-needle carpeted trail through the forest to a ridge offering views to the opposite side of the valley.

Access from I-25 and 6th Ave. Drive west on 6th Ave. to its intersection with Hwys. 6 & 93. Turn right on Hwy. 93, toward Boulder. Drive 1.4 miles and turn left on Golden Gate Canyon Road, marked with a sign for Golden Gate State Park and "White Ranch 10 Miles." Follow Golden Gate Canyon Road to the park entrance. Take your first right and park in the visitor's center.
Drive Time 45-50 minutes

The Hike The Beaver Trailhead is across the road from the park entrance's pay station. A large park map marks the trailhead. From the map, start upward to the left where you'll see a small trail marker. Ignore the sign to Beaver Overlook; it does not connect with the Beaver Trail. In .1 miles, the trail forks. Bear right to start the loop. It goes through a pine forest, parallel to the highway. At about .75 miles, the trail forks again. Head up to the left. The right fork goes downhill, paralleling the highway to Slough Pond. The left fork ascends steeply in a few places but gradually overall for about .75 miles, crossing a small wooden bridge and ascending to the top of a ridge. Here you will see a sign for Beaver Trail Shelter; this is a good place to rest and explore the ridge. Look over the back side for views of the valley. Follow the Beaver Trail as it winds gradually down across an open hillside back the start.

With Kids The Beaver Trail is marked difficult on the park map, but no part should be too steep or unsafe for school-age children. It is fairly long and climbs significantly, however; be prepared.

Trail Notes It costs $5 to enter Golden Gate Canyon State Park.

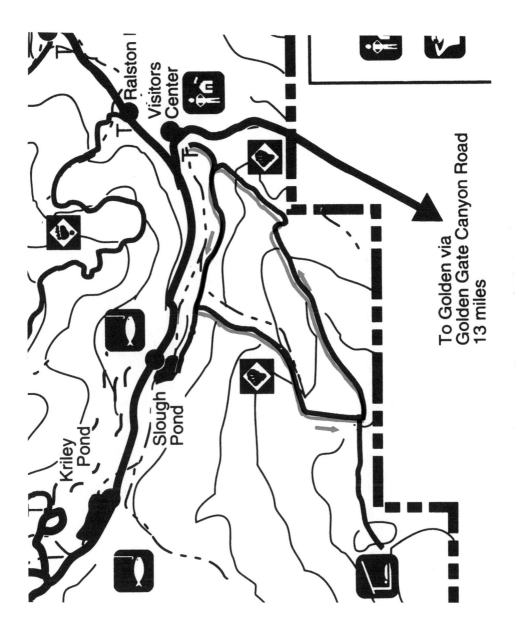

Ralston

Visitors Center

Kriley Pond

Slough Pond

To Golden via
Golden Gate Canyon Road
13 miles

Map by Colorado State Parks

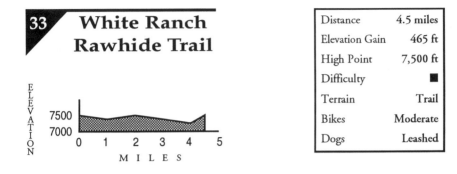

33 White Ranch Rawhide Trail		
Distance		4.5 miles
Elevation Gain		465 ft
High Point		7,500 ft
Difficulty		■
Terrain		Trail
Bikes		Moderate
Dogs		Leashed

Trail Intro A long tour of the north end of White Ranch Park with a little of everything: meadows, forests and panoramic views to the eastern plains.

Access from I-25 and 6th Ave. Drive 12.7 miles west on 6th Ave. to its intersection with Hwys. 6 & 93. Bear right on 93 and continue 1.4 miles to a "White Ranch 10 Miles" sign and turn left. Following the signs to White Ranch Park, turn right in 2.8 miles on Crawford Gulch Road. After 3.8 more miles, turn right on Belcher Hill Road. Drive 1.4 miles to the park entrance and then continue .4 more miles to the 2nd parking lot.
Drive Time 45 minutes

The Hike Begin on the road-width Rawhide Trail. 1.6 miles up, you will intersect the Waterhole Trail. If you need water, there is a pump about 100 feet up this trail. If not, continue along the Rawhide, which narrows to singletrack, crosses a meadow and enters a spruce forest. A brief climb ends at a high viewpoint overlooking Denver and the plains. Continuing, the trail descends sharply to a stream, passes the Wrangler's Run Trail and crosses the stream. From here, it is a half-mile climb to the Longhorn Trail. Upon reaching the Longhorn, stay right and follow the Rawhide Trail back to the start.

Trail Runners This is a solid mid-distance run. After a brief warm-up on a gravelly road, a long climb is followed by a steep, technical descent on a rocky trail. The last hill is a tester; a half-mile-long, 300 foot climb back to the start.

With Kids This is a fairly long hike with a steep climb that may not be suitable for younger children. Be sure older kids are up for it first.

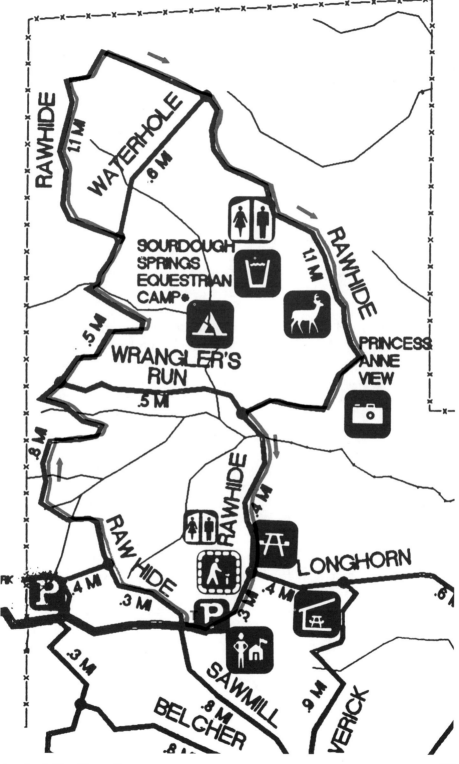

RAWHIDE

WATERHOLE

1.1 M

.6 M

SOURDOUGH
SPRINGS
EQUESTRIAN
CAMP

RAWHIDE

1.1 M

.5 M

WRANGLER'S
RUN

PRINCESS
ANNE
VIEW

.5 M

.8 M

RAWHIDE

.4 M

RAW HIDE

LONGHORN

RK

P

.4 M

.3 M

.4 M

.6 M

.3 M

P

.3 M

.3 M

.9 M

SAWMILL

BELCHER

.8 M

VERICK

.8 M

Distance		4.0 miles
Elevation Gain		520 ft
High Point		8,160 ft
Difficulty		■
Terrain		Trail
Bikes		Moderate
Dogs		Leashed

Trail Intro A meadow loop that climbs through a forest and ends back in the meadow. A longer, more scenic option is to walk to the top of Evergreen Mountain on the Evergreen Mountain Trail West, a 4.6 mile out-and-back that gains 900 feet.

Access from I-25 and 6th Ave. Drive west on 6th Ave. and turn west on I-70. Exit at Evergreen Parkway (Exit #252). Turn left on Hwy. 74 and follow it for 8.4 miles, past Bergen Park, until it intersects Hwy. 73 in the town of Evergreen. Turn right on Hwy. 73. In .7 miles, turn right on Buffalo Park Road. Continue 2.3 miles to the Alderfer/Three Sisters west (the 2nd) parking lot.
Drive Time 45 minutes

The Hike Begin on the Wild Iris Loop. When it intersects the Evergreen Mountain Trail West, turn right and walk to its end where it becomes the Evergreen Mountain Trail East. Follow the East Trail to a junction with the Ranch View Trial and turn left. Turn right on the Wild Iris Loop and return to the start.

Trail Running Smooth trails with gradual ascents and descents. More experienced runners in better shape, looking for a longer route, might try the 7.5K/900 foot out-and-back to the top of Evergreen Mountain.

With Kids This is a very long trail with a fair amount of elevation gain. Try the Brother Loop (#18) instead.

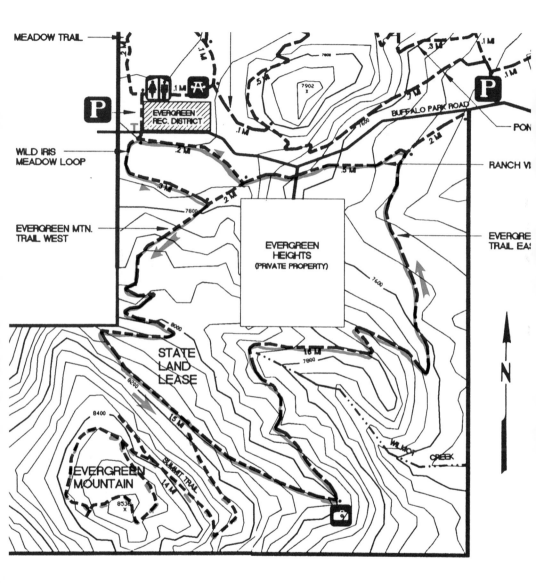

MEADOW TRAIL

P

EVERGREEN
REC. DISTRICT

WILD IRIS
MEADOW LOOP

EVERGREEN MTN.
TRAIL WEST

BUFFALO PARK ROAD

P

PON

RANCH VI

EVERGRE
TRAIL EAS

EVERGREEN
HEIGHTS
(PRIVATE PROPERTY)

STATE
LAND
LEASE

WILMOT
CREEK

SUMMIT TRAIL

EVERGREEN
MOUNTAIN

8535
x

N

Map by Jeffco Open Space

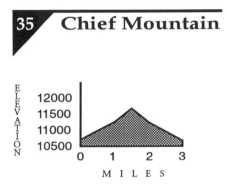

35	**Chief Mountain**		Distance	3.0 miles

Distance	3.0 miles
Elevation Gain	1,000 ft
High Point	11,709 ft
Difficulty	■
Terrain	Trail
Bikes	No
Dogs	Leashed

Trail Intro A soft, pine-needle covered trail through the forest and above tree-line to the summit of Chief Mountain. where a wonderful 360° panorama awaits. My father has made the hike just before dawn, under a full moon, to watch the sunrise from the summit.

Access from I-25 and 6th Ave. Drive west on 6th Ave. and turn west on I-70. Exit I-70 at Evergreen Parkway Exit (#252). Follow Hwy. 74 just past Bergen Park and bear right on Squaw Pass Road (Hwy. 103), following the signs for Mt. Evans and Echo Lake. Continue 12.5 miles up Hwy. 103 until you see a pull off on your right, just past mile marker 19 (you can see an old ski area below the road).
Drive Time 45-50 minutes

The Hike Cross the road to the trailhead (it is signed with a stone marker with the number 290 on it). .2 miles up the trial, cross a jeep road and proceed upward (there is a sign for Chief Mountain on your left). At .5 miles, watch for the trail to switchback upward to the right around a large, flat rock and fallen tree. At .7, trail opens out to beautiful views of Long's, Grey's and Torrey's Peaks, the Indian Peaks and Mt. Audubon. The end of the trail is reached at 1 mile. Here, there are rock outcroppings, places to picnic and spectacular views in every direction.

With Kids When my sister was in 3rd grade, her class hiked to the top of Chief Mountain. There is nothing scary or technical about it, but it does gain a significant amount of elevation in a short distance.

Trail Notes Because of the high elevation this hike attains, you should be in good shape and accustomed to the altitude if you are going to attempt it.

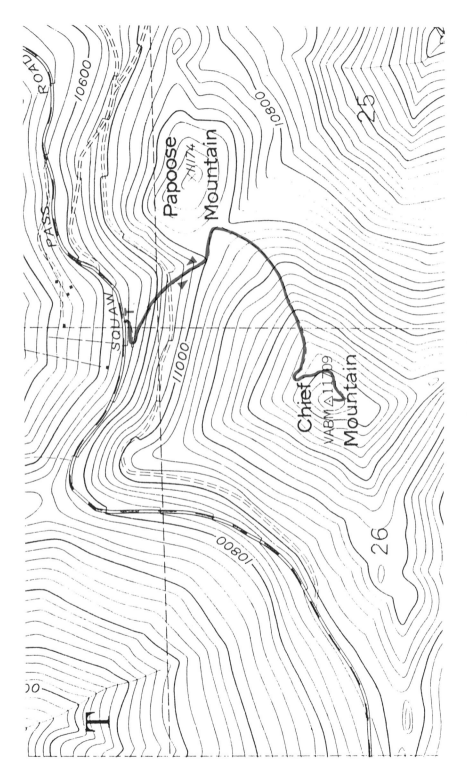

Map by U.S.G.S.

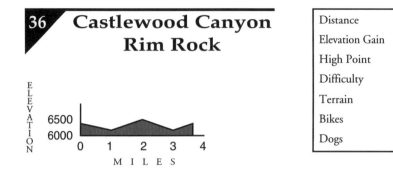

Distance	3.6 miles
Elevation Gain	500 ft
High Point	6,500 ft
Difficulty	■
Terrain	Trail
Bikes	No
Dogs	Leashed

Trail Intro A beautiful, lightly used trail that loops through Castlewood Canyon and past the ruins of the Castlewood Canyon Dam, which broke in 1933 and flooded Denver. The trail then traverses the east rim of the canyon and ends back on the west rim.

Access from I-25 and 6th Ave. Drive south on I-25 toward Colorado Springs. Take the second Castle Rock Exit (#182), following the signs for Hwy. 86 and Franktown. Cross over the highway and take your first right into Castle Rock. Turn left at Fifth Ave. onto Hwy. 86, following the signs for Franktown. In 6.5 miles, turn right on Castlewood Canyon Road (if you reach Franktown, you went too far). Continue for 2.3 miles and park at the Westside Trailhead.
Drive Time 45 minutes

The Hike From the parking lot, descend on the Creek Bottom Trail and turn right when it forks. Descend to Cherry Creek and follow it upstream to a stream crossing at the site of the dam ruins. Climb to the east rim of the canyon and parallel it for just over a mile before dropping back into the canyon. Walk past the Homestead Trail, following the gradually ascending Creek Bottom Trail back to the start.

Trail Running A super run, with a long descent to Cherry Creek followed by a steep climb and decent of the canyon's east rim.

With Kids This is a long and, in places, tough hike, but would be great for more experienced hiking families, especially with the ruins of the dam and Cherry Creek to entertain curious minds. This trail is better in fall as the canyon holds snow in spring and can be hot in summer.

Trail Notes It costs $5 to enter Castlewood Canyon State Park.

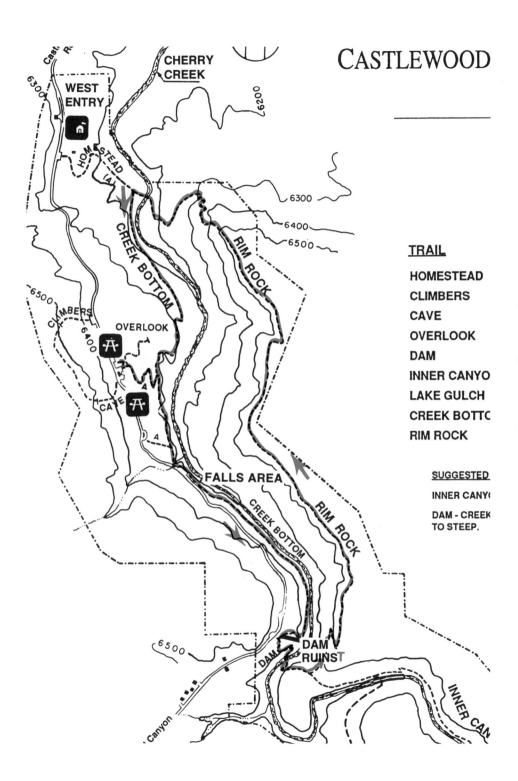

CASTLEWOOD

CHERRY CREEK

WEST ENTRY

HOMESTEAD

CREEK BOTTOM

RIM ROCK

OVERLOOK

CLIMBERS

CAVE

FALLS AREA

RIM ROCK

DAM

DAM RUINS

INNER CAN

Canyon

6300
6200
6300
6400
6500
6500
6400
6500

TRAIL

HOMESTEAD
CLIMBERS
CAVE
OVERLOOK
DAM
INNER CANYO
LAKE GULCH
CREEK BOTTO
RIM ROCK

SUGGESTED

INNER CANYO

DAM - CREEK
TO STEEP.

Union Station - LoDo after the Castlewood Canyon Dam broke in 1933.

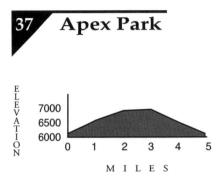

37	**Apex Park**		
		Distance	4.9 miles
		Elevation Gain	800 ft
		High Point	6,960 ft
		Difficulty	■
		Terrain	Trail
		Bikes	Heavy
		Dogs	Leashed

Trail Intro A long, scenic route with views of Denver, Golden and lots of summertime wildflowers. The front side ascent is fairly busy, but the back-side sees far less use.

Access from 6th Ave. and I-70 Drive west on 6th Ave. to Jefferson County Parkway, turn left and follow the brown signs to Apex Park, located next to Heritage Square.
Drive Time 20 minutes

The Hike Walk along the Apex Trail to its intersection with the Sledge Trail. Turn right and uphill onto the Sledge. At the top of the ascent, pass the Pick and Gad Trail, continuing across the front side of the mountain on the Grubstake Loop. You can see Boulder's Flatirons in the far distance to the north. Turn left on the Bonanza Trail. At its end, turn left, and then bear right at a three-way intersection onto the Sluicebox Trail. Switchback down to the Apex Trail, turn left and follow this shady streamside trail back to the start.

Trail Runners A quality route on smooth trails with a long warm-up and a tough climb mid-way. Be careful in summer; this trail can be a scorcher and there's not much shade.

With Kids Between the long distance and the heavy bike traffic, this trail is not recommended for families with children.

Trail Notes You can cut the hike by .8 miles (to 4.1 miles) by turning onto the Pick Trail at the top of the Sledge Trail, instead of taking the longer, more scenic Grubstake and Bonanza Trails

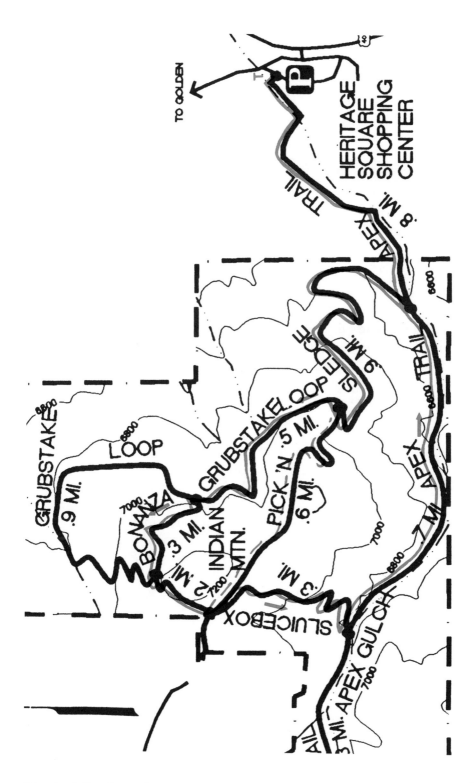

Distance	6 miles
Elevation Gain	700 ft
High Point	6,300 ft
Difficulty	■
Terrain	Trail
Bikes	No
Dogs	Leashed

Trail Intro A popular hike that traces the curves of the foothills above Boulder and ends in a stunning meadow valley with the Flatirons looming above.

Access from I-25 and 6th Ave. Drive north on I-25 then turn west on Highway 36. Follow 36 to the Baseline exit in Boulder. Turn left on Baseline and follow it to Chautauqua Park (on your left between 7th and 8th and Baseline).
Drive Time 40 minutes

The Hike From the Chautauqua parking lot, follow the road-width main trail for about .8 miles and then turn left on the (signed) singletrack Mesa Trail. Stay on the Mesa Trail at all junctions. The trail gradually ascends thorough pine forest before emerging beneath the Flatirons and offering expansive views of the Great Plains to the east (visibility is truly unlimited on a clear day). The trail then switchbacks down to a stream and climbs out into the aforementioned valley. From here, return as you came. (For a longer hike, the trail continues for 4 more miles to Eldorado Springs.)

With Kids The first .8 miles of this hike, along the road-width section of the trail, is very popular with families. Hike as far as you feel the kids are up for and then return as you came.

Trail Running With its moderate climbs, great views and generally smooth surface, this is one of the classic trail runs for all abilities on the Front Range. Less fit runners can run a five mile round trip (as described above to the point where the trail descends to a stream as described above), while the rabbits can run to the end of the trail at the Eldorado Springs road (about 15 miles out-and-back).

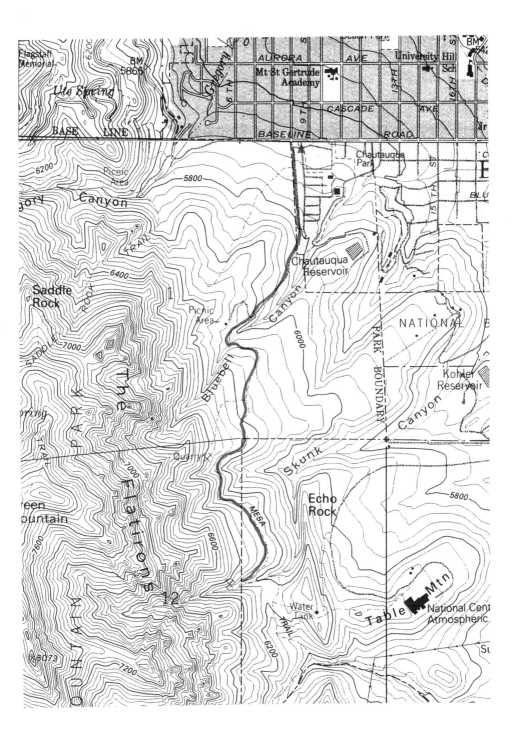

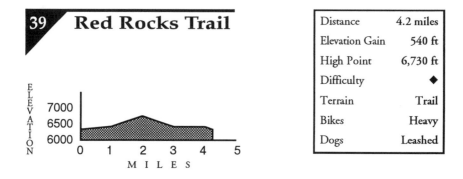

Red Rocks Trail

Distance	4.2 miles
Elevation Gain	540 ft
High Point	6,730 ft
Difficulty	◆
Terrain	Trail
Bikes	Heavy
Dogs	Leashed

Trail Intro Though this trail is one of the busiest on the Front Range, it's still one of my favorites because of the terrain it crosses. Much of the hike is in a high desert ecosystem which traverses rough red sandstone and cactus and yucca desert with greatly contrasting, bright green foliage.

Access from I-25 and 6th Ave. Drive west on 6th Ave. and turn west on I-70. Exit at the Morrison Exit and turn left. Go under I-70 and continue .5 miles to the Matthews/Winters Park parking lot on the right side of the road.
Drive Time 20 minutes

The Hike From the parking lot, join the Village Walk Trail. Head right at a junction just after crossing a bridge and come to another junction in .3 miles. Continue straight (do not bear right) and join the Red Rocks Trail. After crossing a little gulch, turn right on the Morrison Slide Trail and switchback steeply to its summit. There are stellar views of Red Rocks Park along this brief, flat section before you descend. At a junction at the bottom of descent, go straight (the left fork), joining the Red Rocks Trail. Continue past the north end of the Slide Trail, staying on the Red Rocks Trail. Follow the Red Rocks Trail back to the Village Walk Trail junction, bear left onto the Village Walk Trail and return to the start.

Trail Running One of my favorites; tough and beautiful at the same time. A long warm-up is followed by a steep, switchbacking climb and descent.

With Kids Between the long distance and the heavy bike traffic, this trail is not recommended for families with children.

Trail Notes This is an exceptional trail in spring and fall, but it is to be avoided on any hot day; it is totally exposed and bakes just like the desert.

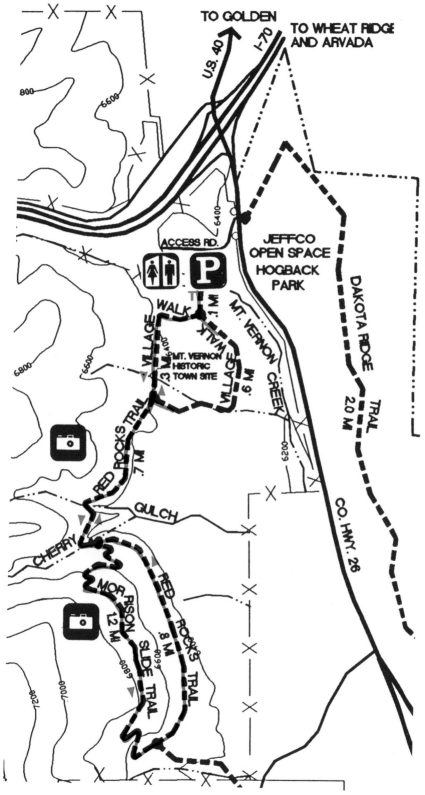

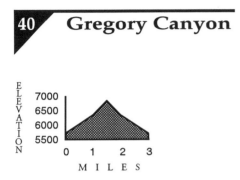

40 **Gregory Canyon**

Distance	3.0 miles
Elevation Gain	1,100 ft
High Point	6,800 ft
Difficulty	◆
Terrain	Trail
Bikes	No
Dogs	Leashed

Trail Intro A popular, rocky (at times) hike that switchbacks up a stunning canyon with the foothills forming the walls of the canyon. In late summer and fall, expect to see signs warning of bear and mountain lion activity in the area. These animals are rarely seen, but are in the area. It is advised to leave dogs behind during these times (or at least they must be leashed).

Access from I-25 and 6th Ave. Drive north on I-25 then turn west on Highway 36. Follow 36 to the Baseline exit in Boulder. Turn left on Baseline and follow it past Chautauqua Park (on your left between 7th and 8th and Baseline). Just before the road takes a hard right, turn left into the Gregory Canyon parking lot (well signed on your left).
Drive Time 45 minutes

The Hike From the Gregory Canyon parking lot, head west on the Gregory Canyon Trail (the trail that starts to the left of the outhouse). The trail follows a stream and climbs very gradually at first among dense green streamside foliage. After crossing the stream on a bridge, the trail climbs much more steeply. Some easy scrambling over rocks follows. Views of the plains, the back of the Flatirons and the 8,144 foot Green Mountain (the green peak on your left (to the south)) emerge as you ascend. At the top of the ascent, the trail merges with an road width trail and leads to an outhouse and picnic area. Return as you came.

Trail Running A tough, rocky run for experienced, fit trail runners.

Trail Notes It costs $3 to park at Gregory Canyon.

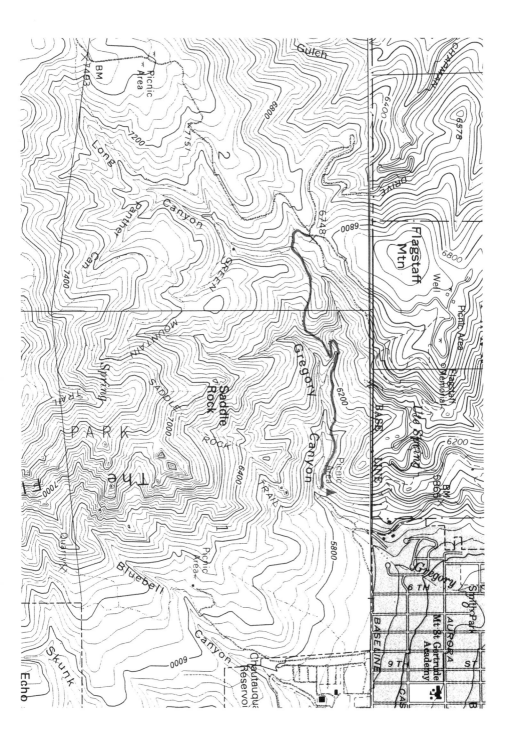

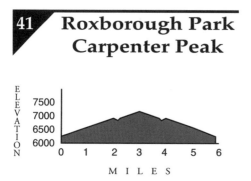

41	Roxborough Park Carpenter Peak		
	Distance	5.8 miles	
	Elevation Gain	1,100 ft	
	High Point	7,175 ft	
	Difficulty	◆	
	Terrain	Trail	
	Bikes	No	
	Dogs	No	

Trail Intro A long, strenuous hike to the top of Carpenter Peak, 1,000 feet above the visitor's center. Tremendous 360° views of the Front Range mountains, the park's famous "red rocks" formations and the city of Denver are your reward

Access from I-25 and 6th Ave. Drive west on 6th Ave. to Wadsworth, turn south and follow it under C-470. 5 miles past C-470, turn left on the Roxborough/Waterton Road. Bear left at the fork and continue on the Roxborough Road to its end at Rampart Range Road. Turn right and follow the signs for another 4.4 miles to the Roxborough Park visitor's center parking lot.
Drive Time 45 minutes

The Hike From the visitor's center, head south on the South Rim Trail. Stay right at a turn-off for the Willow Trail and then turn right onto the Carpenter Peak Trail. Follow the trail across a road and begin ascending steeply into the foothills. A brief flat section is followed by a final push to the top of the peak where you can relax among tall, Stonehenge-like rocks and enjoy the view. Return as you came.

Trail Running A summit run on mostly smooth trails with some rock steps and a few twisty sections that are fun on the descent. A test piece for the serious, in-shape runner. The trail gains 1,000 feet in less than 3 miles (most of it in the last 2 miles), which is tough by most any standard.

Trail Notes It costs $5 to enter Roxborough State Park.

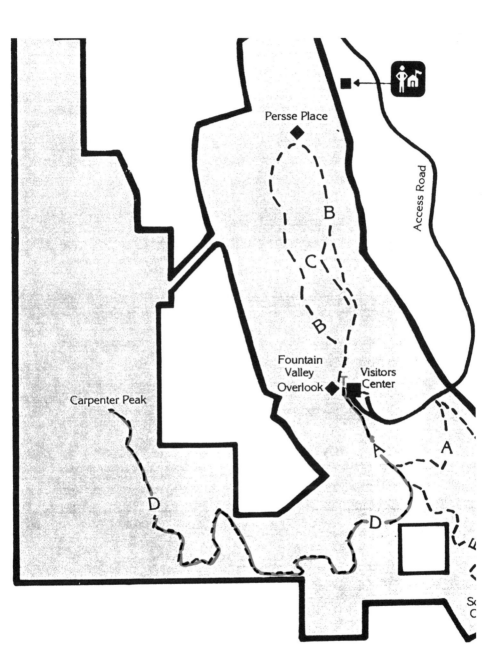

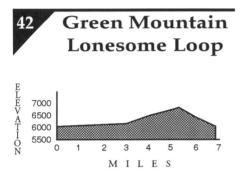

42	**Green Mountain** **Lonesome Loop**	
Distance	6.9 miles
Elevation Gain	800 ft
High Point	6,850 ft
Difficulty	◆
Terrain	Trail
Bikes	Heavy
Dogs	Leashed

Trail Intro A very long and popular trail close to town with wildflower-covered meadows and super Front Range and city views. It is rated advanced because of the length and elevation gain. A better trek in spring and fall than summer, when it can be *very* hot.

Access from I-25 and 6th Ave. Drive west on 6th Ave. and turn west on I-70. Get off at the Morrison Exit and turn left. Go under I-70 and drive 1.4 miles to Hwy. 26 East (across from Red Rocks). Turn left, go up and over the Hogback and turn left on Rooney Road, at the bottom of the hill. Continue .5 miles to the Green Mountain parking lot, on your right.
Drive Time 20 minutes

The Hike Cross the highway on an overpass and bear left on a dirt road which climbs steeply around the north side of Green Mountain. At the top of the ascent look for a little trail on the right which leads to a nice view point. Back on the road, descend very briefly. Intersect a trail and turn right onto it. The trail winds through wildflower-carpeted meadows with views of Red Rocks. As you descend, be alert for bikers approaching from behind. Stay right at a junction with a second trail and continue downhill. At the bottom of the hill, at a 3-way intersection, bear right on the uphill-leading trail and follow it around the east and south side of Green Mountain. Pass several roads and trails, but stay straight at all of these, winding back to the start.

Trail Running My favorite long run close to the city. Loop it counterclockwise to get the big climb out of the way and then enjoy a long cruise on mostly smooth, rolling trail. Can be a scorcher in summer. For experienced trail runners in excellent shape only!

96

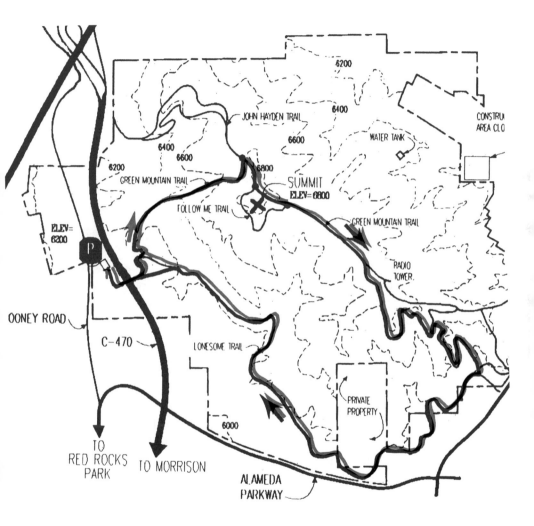

6200

JOHN HAYDEN TRAIL

6400

6600

WATER TANK

CONSTRU
AREA CLO

6400

6600

6200

GREEN MOUNTAIN TRAIL

6800

SUMMIT
ELEV=6800

FOLLOW ME TRAIL

GREEN MOUNTAIN TRAIL

RADIO
TOWER.

ELEV=
6200

P

OONEY ROAD

C-470

LONESOME TRAIL

PRIVATE
PROPERTY

6000

TO
RED ROCKS
PARK

TO MORRISON

ALAMEDA
PARKWAY

Map by Lakewood Parks

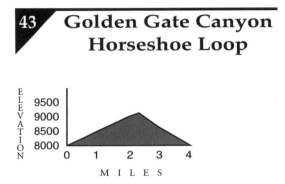

43 Golden Gate Canyon Horseshoe Loop

Distance	4.0 miles
Elevation Gain	1,250 ft
High Point	9,150 ft
Difficulty	◆
Terrain	Trail
Bikes	No
Dogs	Leashed

Trail Intro More mountains than plains, this hike ascends gently at first along a stream and through aspen and pine forest before climbing steeply to a rocky summit with amazing views of the Indian Peaks Wilderness. This is a tough trail for hikers in good shape and used to the altitude.

Access from I-25 and 6th Ave. Drive west on 6th Ave. to its intersection with Hwys. 6 & 93. Turn right on Hwy. 93, toward Boulder, and drive 1.4 miles to Golden Gate Canyon Road, marked with a brown sign for Golden Gate State Park and "White Ranch 10 Miles." Follow Golden Gate Canyon Road to the park entrance. Take your first right, toward the visitor's center. Just past the visitor's center, park at the Ralston Roost trailhead.
Drive Time 45-50 minutes

The Hike Carefully walk up the road for about .2 miles to the Frazier Meadow parking area. Hike up the Horseshoe Trail. Stay left on the Horseshoe Trail at a junction with a horse trail. At a second intersection, turn left onto the Black Bear Trail. Hike more steeply up the Black Bear Trail to a junction with the Mule Deer Trail. Stay left on the Black Bear and hike steeply upward along a rock- and boulder-strewn path to the summit of Ralston Roost. The trail is occasionally hard to follow here but is well signed. (If you are unsure of the direction, look around carefully for trail markers before proceeding). After crossing the summit ridge, descend sharply into the valley back to the start.

Trail Running A tough, very rocky loop with steep ascents and descents. The top of the run is more climbing/walking than running as you negotiate boulder fields and some minor route finding.

Trail Notes It costs $5 to enter Golden Gate Canyon State Park.

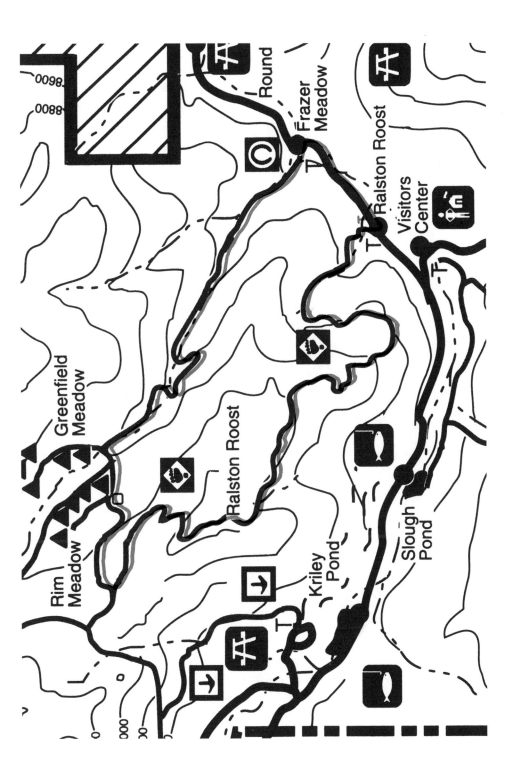

Round

Frazer Meadow

Ralston Roost

Visitors Center

Greenfield Meadow

Ralston Roost

Rim Meadow

Kriley Pond

Slough Pond

0098.

0088.

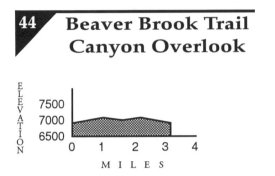

Distance	3.2 miles
Elevation Gain	290 ft
High Point	7,175 ft
Difficulty	◆
Terrain	Trail
Bikes	None
Dogs	Leashed

Intro A 3.2 mile out-and-back along the 6 mile long Beaver Brook Trail leading to a Clear Creek Canyon overlook. This is one of the most difficult trails in the book because of the talus fields to be crossed and several exposed spots where you are climbing through boulders on the edge of a 10-15 foot drop-off. Not for children or those afraid of heights. For competent, experienced hikers only.

Access from I-25 and 6th Ave. Drive 11.7 miles west on 6th Ave. to 19 St. above Golden (the first light after the Jeffco Government Center). Turn left on 19th. In .3 miles, pass through two tall stone columns where 19th becomes Lookout Mountain Road. Continue 3 miles from the columns until you see a parking pull-off on your right and a sign for the Beaver Brook Trail.
Drive Time 30 minutes

The Hike The first part of the trail is shared with the Lookout Mountain Trail. About .2 miles up, stay straight on the Beaver Trail at a junction with the Lookout Mountain Trail. At about .5 miles, and continuing for about .5 miles, is the difficult, rocky part. After that, the trail becomes much easier, following a hillside on a smooth forested trail to a point directly overlooking Clear Creek Canyon. You can turn around here or continue onward and then return as you came when you are ready.

Trail Runners Not a great run as much of the second .5 miles is spent scrambling and clambering over talus fields and boulders. After that it gets good though with rolling forest trail, so if you're looking for a long run (up to 12 miles out-and-back)...

With Kids This is not a good trail for kids because of the exposed areas.

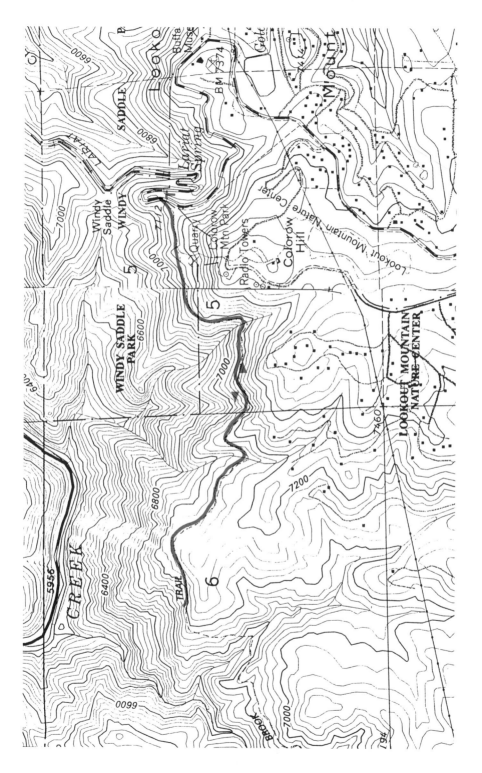

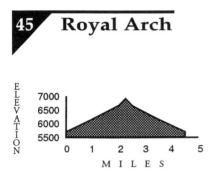

45 Royal Arch

Distance	4.5 miles
Elevation Gain	1,350 ft
High Point	6,950 ft
Difficulty	◆
Terrain	Trail
Bikes	No
Dogs	Leashed

Trail Intro A popular, steep hike to a Moab-like sandstone arch tucked into the famous Flatirons (the red rock outcroppings above Boulder). There are a couple of spots that require a bit of scrambling. You should be in relatively good shape and a confident hiker for this route.

Access from I-25 and 6th Ave. Drive north on I-25 then turn west on Highway 36. Follow 36 to the Baseline exit in Boulder. Turn left on Baseline and follow it to Chautauqua Park (on your left between 7th and 8th and Baseline).
Drive Time 45 minutes

The Hike From the Chautauqua parking lot, follow the road-width main trail uphill. After .8 miles, pass an outhouse and then a picnic shelter. Stay on the road to its end where it intersects the Royal Arch Trail, which is signed. Join the Royal Arch Trail (a left turn) and hike gradually at first through dense green foliage. As the trail ascends more steeply, it enters a densely wooded area. The trail descends briefly and sharply down broken rock steps then climbs steeply to the arch. From the arch are commanding views of the Great Plains to the east (you can see downtown Denver 20 miles away on a clear day!).

Trail Running A grueling, often rocky and steep ascent to a spectacular view point. For fit runners prepared to suffer.

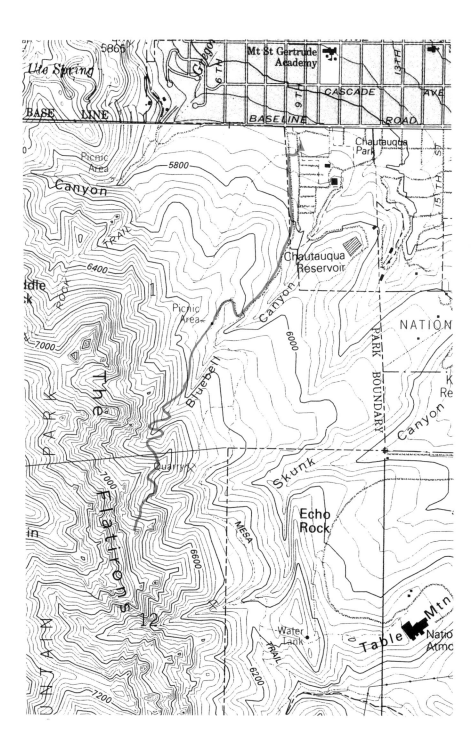